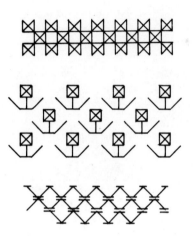

SAMPLERS FOR TODAY

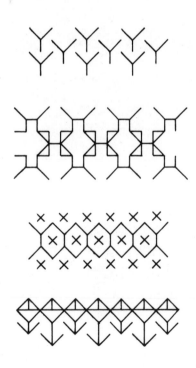

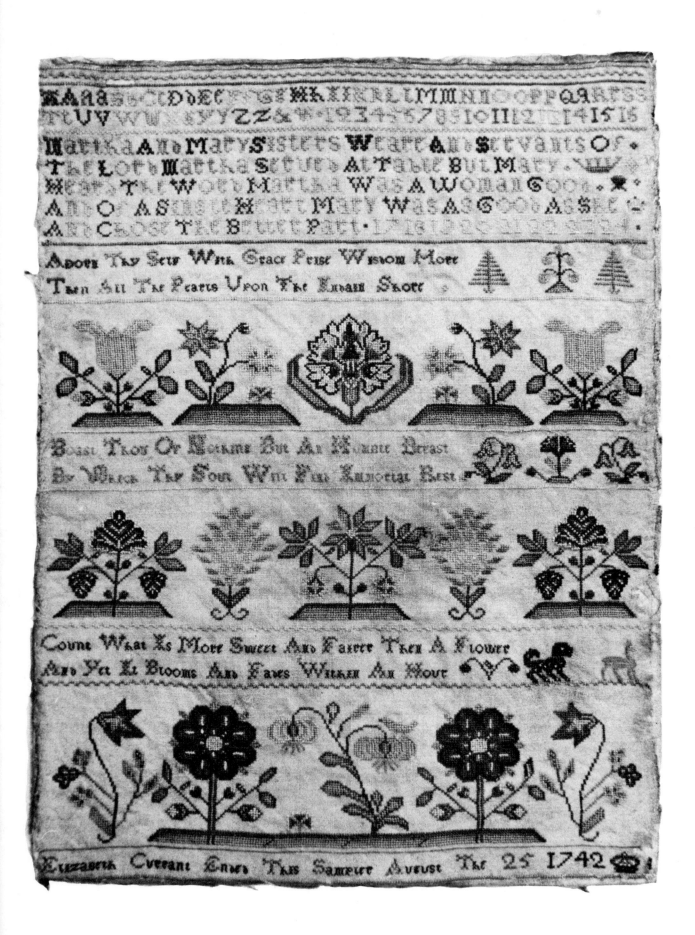

SAMPLERS FOR TODAY

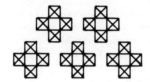

CÉCILE DREESMANN

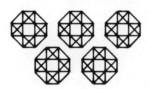

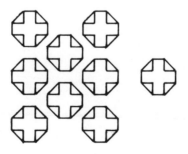

VAN NOSTRAND REINHOLD COMPANY
New York   Cincinnati   Toronto   London   Melbourne

For Anne-Marie

Amongst those who have so generously helped me in my research, I would like to mention the following:

First of all, my husband, without whose constant encouragement and efficient help this book would still be far from completed.

Miss Jacqueline Butler (USA); Miss Constance Howard (England); Mrs. Schipper-van Lottum (the Netherlands); Mrs. Irmgard Johnson (Mexico); Mrs. Norris W. Harkness III (USA); and their excellencies Angel Sans Briz and Livio Theodoli, respectively Spanish and Italian Ambassadors to the Netherlands—all of whom went to so much personal trouble to help me.

The Swiss Heimatwerk and the Danish Haandarbejdets Fremme institutes were of immeasurable assistance. So were the various Embroiderers' Guilds and Women's Institutes from all over the world.

But my thanks go quite as expressly to the literally hundreds of people, individuals and museum authorities, heads of schools, institutions and clubs, who have so generously collaborated to make this book possible.

The author and Van Nostrand Reinhold Company have taken all possible care to trace the ownership of every work reproduced in this book and to make full acknowledgment for its use. If any errors have accidentally occurred, they will be corrected in subsequent editions, provided notification is sent to the publisher.

Van Nostrand Reinhold Company Regional Offices:
New York Cincinnati Chicago Millbrae Dallas
Van Nostrand Reinhold Company International Offices:
London Toronto Melbourne

Copyright © 1972 by Litton Educational Publishing, Inc.
Library of Congress Catalog Card Number 72-1483
ISBN 0-442-22178-9

All drawings of stitches by the author; those on the following pages were drawn by Rino Dussi according to sketches supplied by the author: 26, 27, 35, 40, 49, 54, 57, 64

Designed by Rosa Delia Vasquez
Type set by Drum Lithographers
Printed by Halliday Lithograph Corporation
Color printed by Princeton Polychrome Press
Bound by The Book Press

Published by Van Nostrand Reinhold Company
450 West 33rd Street, New York, N.Y. 10001
Published simultaneously in Canada by
Van Nostrand Reinhold Ltd.
16 15 14 13 12 11 10 9 8 7 6 5 4 3 2 1

Contents

1. Samplers of the Past

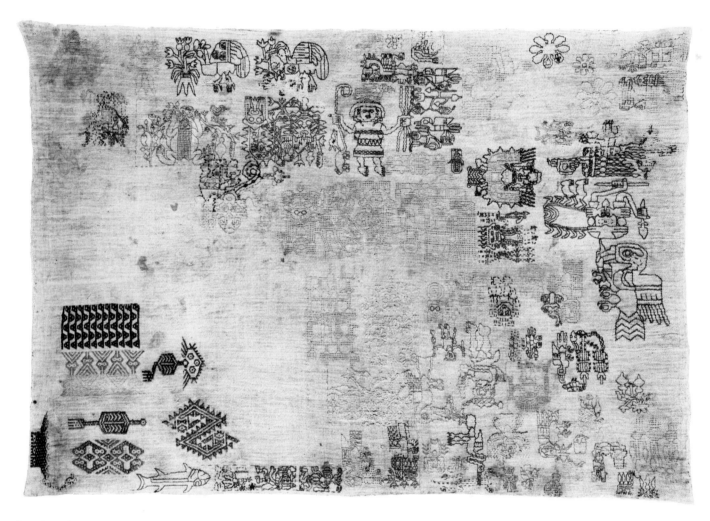

Sampler, circa 200 B.C., early Nazca culture, Peru. Worked on cotton, mainly in straight stitches. (The Museum of Primitive Art, New York City.)

The Beginning

Long before man got to the stage of wearing clothes, he had acquired the habit of decorating his body by either painting motifs on his skin or by incising patterns into it. All such decorations were symbolic in character; all of them carried a message. They were signs meant to obtain the good graces of benevolent gods and to ward off the wrath of evil ones. Their purpose was to protect man against the many physical dangers that surrounded him, and to intimidate his innumerable enemies. Similarly, by wearing the fangs or the skins of animals he had slain, he claimed their strength, their cunning, as his own. Such trophies also clearly demonstrated his prowess as a hunter and his virility.

Much later, on his long and slow road to civilization, man started wearing garments — in some environments to protect himself against the cold; in others, merely to emphasize his status in a community. For whichever reason he covered himself, his doing so meant the ancient symbolical signs were hidden from view; and, believing the signs to have thus lost their power, man then proceeded to reproduce the various symbols on his clothing.

Amongst the means he had at his disposal to do this were the simple utilitarian sewing stitches that he had already invented to hold his garments together, to shape or repair them. Once man started to use these stitches to reproduce the old signs on his clothing, embroidery was born.

Later, in many places, as his sense of security on earth grew, man's impulse to protect himself against all kinds of mysterious dangers diminished. The importance of the symbolical language gradually disappeared from his mind and the embroidered patterns, in time, acquired a purely decorative value. Seafaring, traveling and warfare brought about a growing exchange and dispersion of cultural elements, including textiles and their adornment. There was only one practical way of committing embroidery motifs to memory, of exercising new stitches, or of trying out new technical possibilities, and that was to take a piece of material and use it for that purpose, as a combined reference and exercise sheet. That is how, long ago, the sampler (from the Latin word "exemplar" — example, sample) must have come into being. But although many early poems and manuscripts refer to them, very few actual examples have survived. In our part of the world, it is only from the sixteenth century onward that we are really able to trace the sampler phenomenon continuously and "in the flesh."

Even so, early samplers were often incomplete and were neither signed nor dated. Their purpose was similar to a private recipe book and they were never meant to be "finished." One simply took a new piece of material when no space was left on the previous one.

The main factors that influenced the fantastic growth and popularity of the sampler in the sixteenth century were the Renaissance and the invention of printing.

Painting by Jan Steen, from the collection of the late W.J.R. Dreesmann.

He errs who thinks
Those hands were set
All spinsterlike and cold
That spelt this scarlet alphabet
And birds of blue and gold.

John Drinkwater (1882 – 1937)

7

The Renaissance

The sixteenth century saw tremendous changes, especially in European countries. The new, liberated ideas of the Renaissance permitted a previously unknown concentration on the pleasures of physical existence. Rapidly expanding trade with foreign countries brought new riches to many more people than hitherto had had access to any form of luxury. Newly imported fabulous silks and velvets, adorned with stitchery and with gold and precious stones, were used to cover bodies that were neither habitually clean nor free of all sorts of festering wounds and infections. This, in turn, brought about the use of linen underwear, originally intended to protect the dress material rather than the wearer.

Initially modest and simple, this underwear soon began to show a decoration at neck and wrist. The use of ever-larger and more spectacular collars and cuffs led to the invention of new kinds of decorative stitchery. These embroideries had to be equally attractive in front and back, since — more often than not — both sides of the collars, cuffs, and ruffles were visible. The simple black-on-white, two-sided decorations that Holbein immortalized in his paintings were gradually replaced by transparent effects obtained through withdrawal of threads — first in one direction, later in both directions of the material.

Sixteenth-century Italian sampler, silk on linen, in straight and long-armed stitches. (The Victoria and Albert Museum, London, England.)

Jane Seymour, third wife of Henry VIII, as painted by Hans Holbein the Younger. The frills at the wrists clearly show the so-called Holbein work. (Mauritshuis, The Hague, the Netherlands).

Seventeenth-century Italian sampler, signed
Gullia Piccolomini, showing the gradual trans-
formation of embroidery into needle lace.
(Victoria and Albert Museum, London,
England.)

As general opulence among the higher strata of Renaissance society grew, so did the taste for luxury. Garments were smothered with embroidery and with gold and precious stones. Adornments at neck and wrists grew into fabulous lacy structures. More and more threads were drawn out of, or cut away from, the linen — the spaces becoming filled with lacelike patterns until no more was left of the linen background than a token support. Finally, this support proved superfluous; a new system came into being: The decorative stitchery was worked over guide threads that were attached to a background material over an intervening sheet of waxed paper, which carried the design. The waxed paper was removed and the background material was cut away upon completion of the stitchery. Since embroidery is basically the adornment of an already existing material, this newly born "needle lace" left the domain of stitchery to join the arts of textile making, like weaving, bobbin lace, knitting and macramé.

Man's collar, early seventeenth century, probably Italian; intricate drawn-thread work and needle lace. The patterns in the many squares form a sampler in their own right. (Rijksmuseum, Amsterdam, the Netherlands.)

Not only did "luxuries-to-wear" become more readily available, the households themselves grew to contain more and more, finer and finer linen. Tablecloths, pillows, and cushions were lavishly embroidered. So were curtains, chairs and boxes, until hardly any textile or textile-covered object was without its gold, silver and silk stitchery, its pearls and precious stones, its fine, drawn-thread work or lace.

Gradually, the linen cupboards filled to overflowing and ownership markings in the forms of crowns, coats of arms or just initials became a necessity. All these new forms of embroidery were reflected in the sixteenth and seventeenth century samplers: the black and white, the gold and silver, the lacy patterns, the crowns, and the lettering.

Early seventeenth-century English painting of Elizabeth, Countess of Southampton, at her dressing table. The overabundance of decoration is clearly shown on her clothing, on curtains, cushions, and tablecloth. (By kind permission of His Grace the Duke of Buccleuch and Queensberry).

The Pattern Books

Pattern books, which exercised an enormous influence on European embroidery, first appeared in the early sixteenth century. Italian and German, French and English artists made the designs for them. Some of these pattern books included counted-thread work as well as cutwork and needle-lace designs. They often remained famous and in great demand for centuries: Giovanni Vavasore's *Essemplario di Lavori* (1530), Johann Sibmacher's *Schön neues Modelbuch* (1597), Richard Shorleyker's *A Scholehouse for the Needle* (1624), and many others. Some patterns, published in England under the title of *The Needle's Excellency,* had had more than ten reprints by the middle of the seventeenth century and were still being printed in Germany as late as 1885.

Part of this long-lasting popularity was no doubt due to the fact that the counted-thread patterns could be executed in a variety of techniques: in cross-stitch and tent stitch, in beadwork, and also in drawn-thread and filet work.

The wide circulation and the long lifespan of the sampler book make geographical and historical identification of a sampler sometimes extremely difficult, unless it is signed and dated. Even then, one wonders how many not-so-very-young women may have felt it wise to make a slight alteration in the date of her childhood sampler!

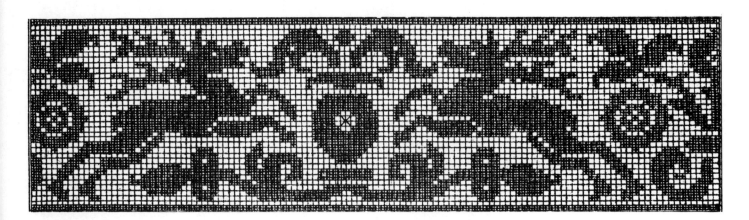

Pattern from Johann Sibmacher's *Schön neues Modelbuch,* 1597.

Sampler Pictures

Queens kept samplers as reference sheets for their ladies-in-waiting to work from. Professional embroiderers used them to permit their patrons an extensive choice of decorations. Soon children were taught the making of samplers and teaching systems were developed for that purpose.

The children would spent the first year learning to embroider alphabets and simple cross-stitch patterns. The next year they might be taught more complicated openwork and a generally finer execution of a greater variety of stitches. For the children, sampler making became not only an exercise, but a proof of talent and competence, of neatness and discipline, and the product was proudly signed and dated upon completion.

The initially scattered motifs and simple, successive rows of patterns were gradually replaced by more complicated and representational compositions and a "framing border" was introduced. Storytelling elements made their appearance and the sampler slowly acquired an added context, that of a "sampler picture."

Early seventeenth-century English sampler, worked with silver and silver gilt thread with sequins and silks on linen, in a great variety of stitches. The museum where this sampler is kept also possesses a pincushion worked with parts of exactly the same pattern. (The Victoria and Albert Museum, London, England.)

In many West European countries, religious strife was the order of the day and strongly affected people's lives. Under such influences, the embroidery hours gradually became coupled to religious indoctrination and, consequently, countless pious verses were worked into samplers. Elizabeth Currant embroidered in 1742:

"Martha and Mary sisters we are and servants of the Lord
Martha served at table but Mary heard the word
Martha was a woman good and of a simple heart
Mary was as good as she and chose the better part."

English sampler, dated 1742; finely worked cross-stitches and tent stitches in silk on canvas. (Author's collection.)

Often, in the later part of the seventeenth century and through the early part of the nineteenth century, samplers included heavily moralizing verses, the likes of which would cause a shudder amongst present-day educators and psychologists. Fourteen-year-old Margaret Morgan, a Welsh girl, was made to embroider in 1839:

"There is an hour when I must die
Nor can I tell how soon twill come
A thousand children, young as I
Are call'd by Death to hear their doom."

Welsh sampler dated 1839; in various stitches with silk on canvas. (National Museum of Wales, Cardiff, Wales.)

Gradually, the double potential of the embroidery lessons was further exploited to include geography lessons, exercises in arithmetic, all sorts of genealogical trees and mourning pictures, commemorative samplers and embroidered family stories. As the storytelling element became more and more important, and as less emphasis was put on the technical exercise as such, it became increasingly difficult to determine what really still was some sort of a sampler and what should be called an embroidered picture.

Then, in the early nineteenth century, a phenomenon called Berlin Woolwork arrived on the scene. A Berlin merchant invented and marketed new embroidery pattern presentations, color printed on square paper. Aided by their extensive reproduction in the new ladies' journals, these patterns rapidly inundated both Europe and the United States. Originally meant to be executed in woolen yarn on canvas, the naturalistic motifs were eventually also used for beadwork and the working of finer cross-stitch patterns on linen. In Vienna, an art dealer by the name of Heinrich Muller published another 3,000 embroidery pattern sheets, slightly more delicate and a little lighter in style than the German patterns.

"Perpetual Almanack" embroidered in silk on cotton in cross-stitches and eyelet stitches, English, 1787; signed by Elizabeth Knowles. Note that the motifs at bottom, left and right, are identical or reversed repeats. (Victoria and Albert Museum, London, England.)

The Many Faces of the Sampler

It would be wrong to consider "our" sampler a purely European and North American matter. Samplers were produced all around the Mediterranean Sea, for instance, also in Mexico and many South American countries. Nor has sampler making ever become purely and solely a children's task. Adults, professionals as well as amateurs, have always continued making them.

Late nineteenth-century Persian sampler, worked in silks on linen. (Metropolitan Museum of Art, New York City. Gift of Mrs. Russell Sayer, 1916.)

Sampler in silks on linen showing delicate
darning patterns and very finely worked cross-
stitch motifs, dated 1857. (Author's collection.)

Berlin Woolwork cross-stitch sampler (but worked in silk) bearing Dutch flag and coat of arms of the city of Amsterdam, dated 1856. (Author's collection.)

Early eighteenth-century French engraving of a lady working at her sampler. (Author's collection. Photograph by Bert Buurman.)

The sampler has taken many shapes, from the scroll-type ones that were meant to be kept in a work box (those were often quite large and sometimes well over a yard long) to tiny sample books with each page a miniature sampler carefully sewn onto the paper. Some samplers were hung on the wall; others were mounted on cushions or other objects for daily use. Some also found their way onto costumes. England's Queen Elizabeth I showed off the success of her explorers in an outsized sampler-type embroidery that was worked on the front part of her skirts. In many countries, embroidered parts of the regional costume told a story about the wearer or indicated his or her identity. And even today, several of the still-existing, purely tribal forms of dress show analogous characteristics.

Portrait of Queen Elizabeth I, covered in jewels, lace, and embroidery. The front part of her skirt shows a variety of plants and herbs, birds and animals, symbolizing the successful ventures of her ships abroad and the ensuing prosperity during her reign over England. (Hardwick Hall, Derbyshire, England.)

Fisherman's wife from Urk, the Netherlands, wearing an "identification" sampler as part of her costume, 1913. (Het Nederlands Openluchtmuseum, Arnhem, the Netherlands.)

Towards the end of the nineteenth century, in our parts of the world, sampler production became impoverished and deteriorated. Just what caused this is hard to say. The invention of the sewing machine, a growing emphasis on the sciences in school education and, later of course, two successive world wars helped form a period wherein few samplers of any merit or attraction were produced. It is after the second world war, in this standardized, mechanized age of ours, that samplers have come into their own again.

All over the world, adults are taking a renewed interest in the making of samplers to tell a personal story, to show mastery of their chosen form of stitchery, or to make a "sample" of work to come. The sampler, that rather fabulous expression of the individual, has definitely started a new career.

Woman's blouse from Oaxaca, Mexico, embroidered on cotton with various finely worked borders and bird motifs in red, combined with a multi-colored, storytelling sampler strip. (Museum of the American Indian, Heye Foundation, New York City.)

Pure exercise samplers in both counted-thread and free embroidery, made by students at the Embroiderers' Guild in Sydney, Australia. Top exercises by Ann Marie Bakewell; bottom left and right by Prue Socha.

Collected with much praise and in-
dustrie,
From scorching Spaine and freezing
Muscovie
From fertile France and pleasant Italie
From Poland, Sweden, Denmarke, Ger-
manie,
And some of these rare patterns have
been set
Beyond the boundes of faithless
Mahomet,
From spacious China and those King-
domes East
And from great Mexico in Indies West.
Thus are these works farre fetch't and
dearly bought,
And consequently good for ladyes
thought.

This seventeenth century poem holds literal truth for today: Examples for this book came from all corners of the earth, proving amply and beyond the shadow of a doubt how intense and universal present-day interest in sampler making is. Intense and universal, but above all diversified; hardly a technique exists for which some sampler was not presented. So many beautiful, interesting, out of the ordinary, and often touching story-telling ones arrived at my writing table that it was often extremely difficult to pick and choose amongst such a wealth of material.

As it stands, *Samplers for Today* tries to give as adequate a survey as possible of all the different aspects of present-day sampler making — the traditional as well as the wildly experimental; the touching human story, often very simple in its technical aspects, as well as examples of great professional perfectionism. It also draws comparisons with analogous sampler work from many different parts of the world. In a few cases, old samplers are shown either because their quality is far superior to the present-day product, or because I feel that they offer a special incentive, a source of inspiration, un-available elsewhere.

All needlework can be categorized in several ways. A particular embroidery, for instance, can be identified according to one of the many existing needlework techniques, such as canvas work or blackwork, each of which has its own characteristics. These techniques are described in Chapter 4. An embroidery could also be identified according to whether the stitches have been worked in either of two basic ways — by using counted threads of the material as a precise guideline for the stitches, or by using the material merely as a back-ground for freely placed stitches. Samplers, however, can also be categor-ized in another way, and that is accor-ding to the work's primary function — whether it is to explore and display the many possibilities of a particular tech-nique or whether it is to tell a story. I have, therefore, divided the samplers into two main groups: technical exercise samplers and storytelling samplers.

A technical exercise sampler can con-sist of straightforward, basic stitchery, or it can consist of experiments and exer-cises in a particular technique. Some technical samplers are worked along the counted-thread method and some are done entirely in free embroidery. There are also technical samplers that combine counting threads with free embroidery and some that tell a story at the same time.

Storytelling samplers can also be worked in free embroidery or by the counted-thread method, and they can have many different faces — relating the story of a family, of a country, or of a hobby, for example — but the emphasis is generally on pictorial or informative content rather than on technical exer-cises. Between these two sampler groupings, and mixed in with them as well, are various embroideries depicting alphabets and genealogical trees, and embroideries that have other aspects relating them to samplers.

Whichever kind of sampler you are going to play with, experiment or study with, prove your dexterity with, or tell your story with, please, please, be sure to sign and date it on completion.

The oldest sampler known to date that men-tions the year in which it was made (1598) and the worker's name: Jane Bostocke. (Courtesy Victoria and Albert Museum, London, England.)

Counted-Thread Embroidery

Samplers that show basic stitches worked by counting the threads of the background material in some way generally present one or more of the following characteristics: 1. Stitches that are worked in straight rows — either horizontal, vertical, or diagonal ones. 2. Stitches that form a "filling." These fillings can consist of a series of independent motifs scattered on the material, or they can be a series of lines that form a network (almost like a second, fancy weave) over the background material.

In the early glamour-time of the sampler, the sixteenth century and the beginning of the seventeenth, the linear and angular qualities of the designs can already be quite clearly observed, for they correspond to the basic possibilities of all counted-thread work.

Sometimes this kind of technical exercise is combined with an alphabet or with exercises in pulled fabric or drawn-thread work.

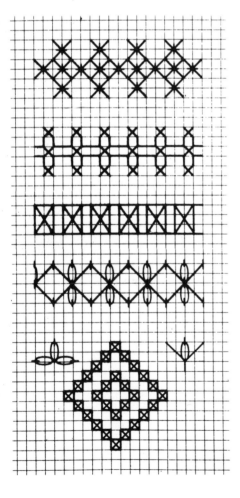

Details of counted-thread embroideries shown on pages 68, 95, and 104.

Free Embroidery

Free embroidery exercises are built on an entirely different concept, for now the material forms a background only and the stitches follow free-flowing lines, independent of the weave of the material.

Again, in this kind of sampler, different "systems" can be distinguished. The designed forms can be filled entirely (by satin stitching or chain stitching, for example) or the designed forms can have fillings not unlike those of counted-thread samplers, except that now the shape, size and direction of the stitches are determined by the eye alone.

In quite a few cases, free embroidery and counted-thread work are combined in one sampler. In some areas, the worker uses the weave of the background to obtain the desired effects, while in other areas the weave is ignored and an imaginary or pre-designed free line is followed.

It may be useful, while perusing the following pages, to bear these purely technical essentials in mind. Technical awareness helps train one's eye, for one thing, and it is also useful in trying to find out exactly why one design seems much more attractive than another, why one kind of work seems so much more exciting than the next. In short, it will help identify one's personal tastes and preferences.

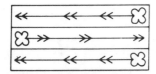

Details of free embroideries shown on pages 58, 75, and 123.

Technical Exercise Examples

Dividing the material into squares is a favorite method for working a true technical exercise sampler. Here are two Dutch examples. The very intricate one below (in rust and brown colors on natural, woven linen) is formed into 136 squares, all beautifully, faultlessly worked. The result: a fabulous wall decoration with a severe, geometrical air about it that would fit into the most modern of homes. The maker of this piece is Mrs. Oudshoorn of The Hague, the Netherlands, and it is owned by Mrs. Bos-de Jong of Dordrecht, also in the Netherlands.

Lighter in vein and involving considerably less work is a smaller sampler (right) by one of my former pupils, whose name I can recall only in part: "Truus." I know she will forgive me for including her so incompletely named, as I felt her sampler to be clear-cut and delicate, yet a project within reach of many. The sampler, measuring approximately 18 x 23 inches, was worked by her in white on fine, pale blue, even-weave linen.

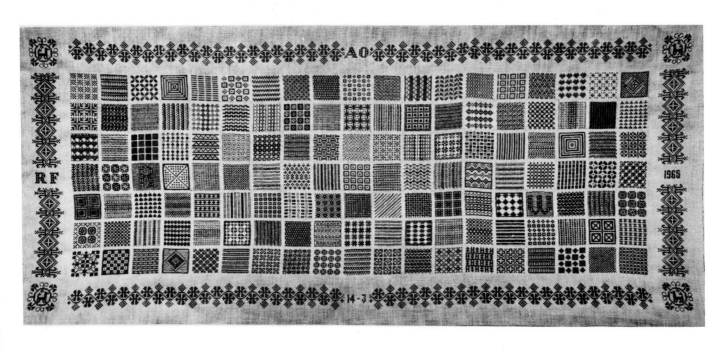

It took me five years of leisure time to complete the white-work sampler showing 150 different varieties of stitches and fillings, in white thread on fine, white linen. There are 90 squares surrounded by drawn-thread work. Various kinds of thread were used; with the exception of some leaf shapes in free embroidery, most of the work was done by counting threads.

A labor of love, dating from my own teaching years (1946-1951), the sampler was at the same time a sort of proof of the mastering of a chosen craft, which is why such things were called "masterpieces" in the days of the guilds. I must confess that I would be both unable and unwilling to undertake a similar project again! Its size: 18 x 46 inches.

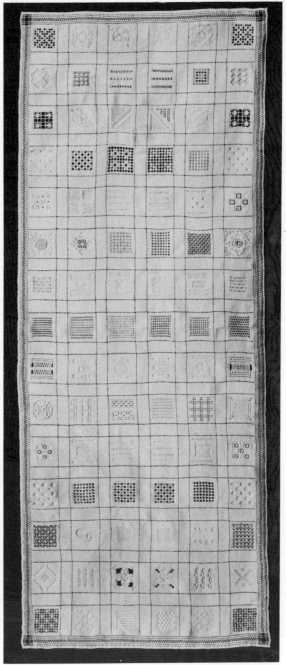

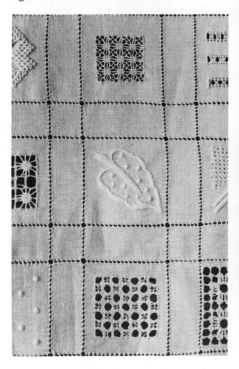

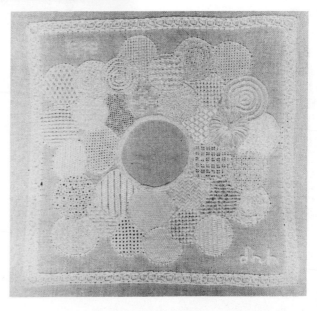

Coins of different sizes were used by Mrs. Norris Harkness III, of New York City, as forms for this very delicate exercise in drawn-thread stitchery.

A division into squares is also used for this present-day sampler cloth from Leukas, an island along the west coast of Greece. The embroidery, on linen, shows an openwork style in white on white that is typical for the island and is called "Carysianico." These patterns decorate the neck and sleeves of both men's and women's costumes.

The variety of embroidery techniques used in Greek regional costumes is almost unbelievable; the Benaki Museum, in Athens, alone houses such an enormous wealth of Greek embroideries that a year's dedicated study might not suffice to acquire a comprehensive knowledge of the literally hundreds of different techniques used. It should be borne in mind, of course, that the Turks, during their centuries-long occupation of what is now Greece, introduced many Near Eastern patterns — while, on the islands, a great many pirates took refuge, bringing with them, as part of their loot, embroidery influences from all over the seafaring world.

It is interesting to compare the incredibly fine work in this nineteenth-century shirt from Leukas with the coarser, twentieth-century version seen on the sampler from the same Greek island. (Shirt from the Benaki Museum, Athens, Greece. Photo of sampler courtesy of National Organization of Hellenic Handicrafts, Athens, Greece.)

Other localities also have characteristic techniques. Some time after the second world war, a group of women from Dorset, England, got together and adapted basic, old local stitches into a form of embroidery called "Dorset Feather Stitchery." Subsequently, after successful experimentation, this work was written up in a book published under that name; and, indeed, featherstitches, together with chain stitches and buttonholing, form the backbone of this experiment. Some of the charming motifs published in the book were incorporated by Jo Hak-Kerkhoven, of the Netherlands, on a sampler of white and pale blue linen. The sampler also shows a variety of openwork, and rows and squares from other sources, such as the famous Norwegian "Hardanger" work.

The designing and making of embroidery is not purely a woman's domain by any means. In the old days, even in western Europe, the "court embroiderer" held a position similar to that of a "court goldsmith." Many techniques, such as goldwork and velvet appliqué were often exclusively executed by professional embroiderers. Most of the pattern books were the work of male artists. Even today, in many countries, specific types of embroidery are traditionally done by men only, while the women tend to confine themselves to such techniques as drawn-thread work, white work and the execution of initials.

As the works of Louis J. Gartner, Jr., and Charles Quaintance, Jr., show, American men have caught on to the present fashion of needlepoint and have done so fast, effectively, and intensively.

Lajos Erdei from Derecske, Hungary, is one of that country's most famous present-day *szür* embroiderers. *Szürs* are the fabulous coats which the shepherds wear.

A needlepoint frame for a mirror was designed by Louis J. Gartner, Jr., who also wrote an excellent book on needlepoint.

Patchwork canvas sampler, mounted for use in a director's chair, was designed by Mr. Charles Quaintance, Jr. (Photograph courtesy of Alice Maynard, Inc., New York City.)

Canvas work is a type of stitchery that relies mainly on counted-thread work. Mrs. Clinton B. Burnett — a longtime, fervent and perfectionist embroideress — worked a clever doorstop in which she incorporated her favorite canvas filling stitches. The background is red with black stripes, the fillings are in white, pale blues and yellows, producing a strong, sun-filled, exhilarating effect.

This is an ideal, not too ambitious nor time-consuming project for a non-designer, but it will prove useful to give the color composition a good deal of thought before starting out. It might also be a good plan to make cut-outs in paper of the top of the doorstop (an ordinary, good-sized brick can be used) and of its four standing sides. Plan the squares, stripes, or other shapes on the cut-outs and add the colors in crayon — this will prevent possible future disappointment.

Canvas work is a favorite subject for Mrs. Muriel Baker, of Farmington, Connecticut, who has been teaching, designing, and lecturing about embroidery for over fifteen years. This sampler and those on the next page were made for teaching purposes, which is why the backgrounds have not been filled in.

The abstract piece, which looks as though it were composed of swatches from a sample book, is Mrs. Baker's own invention, and it would make a very striking wall decoration for a modern home or for a man's den. Just imagine it with the background filled in and with your own favorite stitches and colors.

Like Mrs. Burnett's doorstop, this is a wonderful project (adaptable to any size) for anyone who likes abstracts — or for anyone who just does not feel up to intricate, naturalistic designs and yet wants to be an independent, creative needle-pointer.

33

The two animal samplers were developed by Mrs. Baker after initial designs by Barbara Ayre. Both samples show a great variety of canvas stitches and it is interesting to compare this version of a turtle with the color example on page 42.

In all three of Mrs. Baker's works, a color scheme of different shades of blue has been used, which gives the pieces a very subtle, unusual appeal.

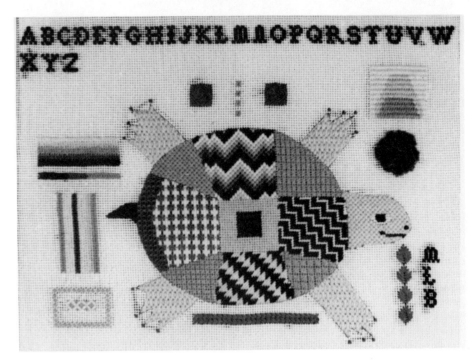

Another needleworker, Mrs. Betty Robison, who teaches crewel and canvas work in Sand Lakes, New York, has been a needlework and general craft buff all her life; she still has in her possession some pictures that she did when she was eight years old, and some forty years from being the professional embroideress and teacher she now is.

"Crazy Quilt" is the name of the canvas sampler by Mrs. Robison; the effect is emphasized by the open chain stitches (in embroidery silk) that surround each element in the sampler, which measures 20 x 16 inches. The accompanying drawing has been kindly put at my disposal by her.

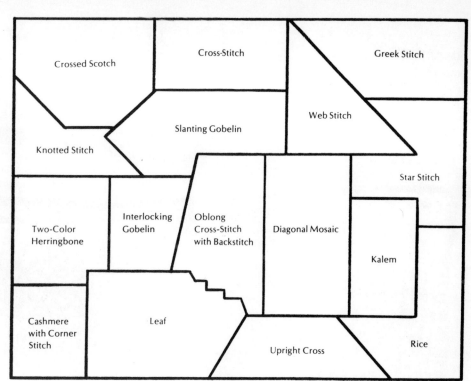

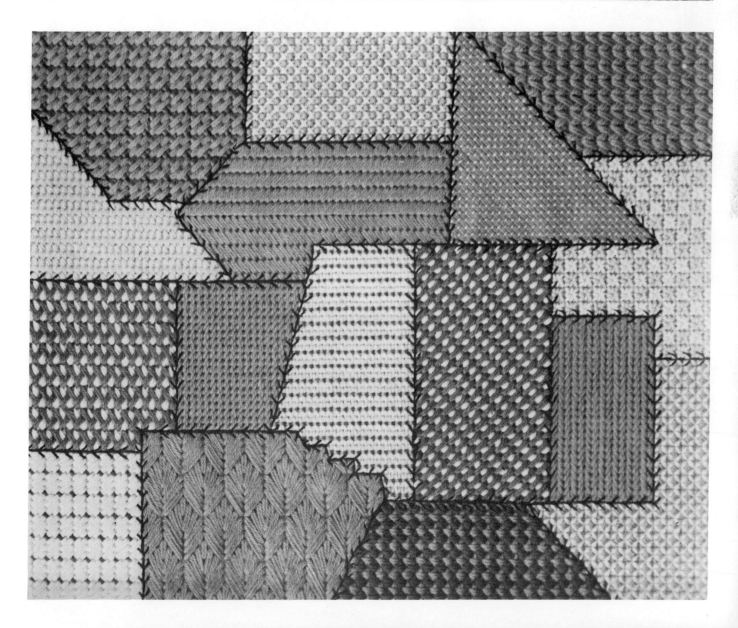

Cushion by Mrs. John McKinlay.

Cushions are a favorite use to which canvas-work samplers are put. Two American "addicts" are Mrs. John McKinlay of Chicago and Mrs. William Golden of New York.

Mrs. McKinlay, whose mother taught her embroidery when she was a child, stayed with this early hobby and, via years of doing different kinds of stitchery, finally decided that needle-point was her favorite. Being a very inventive and active woman, she soon became bored with the classical "tent-stitch-only" method, and she started to experiment on her own. Her first pillow sampler (see opposite page), in shades of gray with white and black, gave her the idea of exploring the decorative values of the *wrong* side of these stitches, and she has since made a specialty of that.

Like Mrs. Baker, Mrs. McKinlay likes to work in shades of one color only and feels that the greatest challenge of canvas samplers is in making the different patterns fit naturally into each other.

Mrs. Golden, who is also a longtime and ardent needlepointer, got the inspiration for this particular sampler cushion from a Mondriaan painting. She used about a dozen different stitches, with a pale lemon-yellow as the basic color and accents in two shades of green and yellow.

Mrs. John Labis and her mother, Mrs. Miriam Richardson of Wales, Massachusetts, have made these quite fantastic canvas samplers of bargello work, which look like optical illusions. Based on straight, vertical stitches covering a canvas background, bargello is a very old technique that, once more, is acquiring a rapidly growing group of fans these days.

Very often there is a wavelike effect to the patterns (due to judicious spacing of stitches, combined with changing colors for each row), which also go under the name of flame stitch, Florentine and Hungarian work.

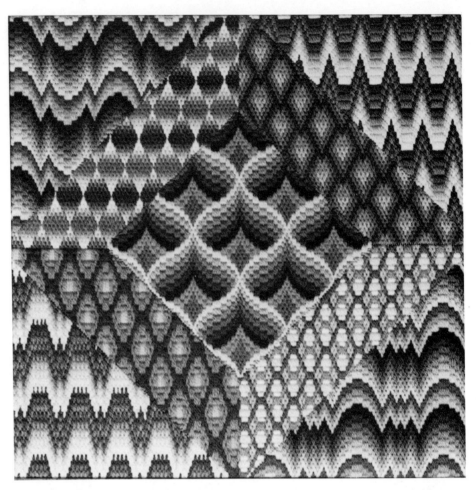

Mrs. J. Bushnell Richardson Jr.'s bargello sampler measures 13 x 13 inches and is worked in shades of red and blue; the colors are combined in each of the nine different patterns.

Mrs. John J. Labis's bargello sampler also measures 13 x 13 inches; it has a center pattern in brick colors, surrounded by golds, olives, and a recall of the brick shades used.

Very much of a perfectionist, Mrs. Labis worked the back of her ten-pattern sampler every bit as neatly as the front.

An old, very traditional sampler motif is "the ship with men." In the sampler here, Dutch ceramist Greetje Petri-Eyskoot, who designs and makes samplers as a hobby, started with the traditional motif and surrounded it with a fabulous collection of self-invented animals. The text is a Dutch translation of a Chinese poem and most of the geometrical patterns are of her own design as well. Married to a sculptor, Mrs. Petri lives and works in an old farmhouse in the eastern part of Holland.

Mrs. Petri very kindly allowed me to select one of her very delightful animal designs for reproduction. It has been simplified for work in one color and the effect should be stunning in red or black on white — or even in white on a vivid green or blue.

Sampler by Greetje Petri-Eyskoot of the Netherlands, 1958. Mellow and complementary colors on natural linen; size approximately 30 x 37 inches.

Many old samplers, mainly those that were made where and when damask linen tablecloths were the fashion, contain pattern darning. Girls would be taught on a sampler the reconstruction of intricate damask weaves for repair purposes. They were made to do the darns in variously colored threads so that no mistake could escape the teacher's stern eye. (See the historical example in color on page 18.)

Rare are those who still enjoy doing this kind of exercise. The delightful little sampler here has a centerpiece taken from a nineteenth-century Viennese pattern, and the maker (whose age you can tell by looking at her year of birth indicated above the central panel) is Jo Hak-Kerkhoven of Amsterdam, who worked with me for many years while I was still teaching in Holland.

Blackwork sampler picture in the traditional manner, made by Dorothy Haeger of Scotland in 1925. (Courtesy of the Gray's School of Art, Aberdeen, Scotland.)

A very delicately worked sampler in black on natural scrim with added details of gold thread. The two little snails form a lively interruption of the mostly traditional motifs. The work is by Edith Gorringe and is part of the collection of The Embroiderers' Guild in London, England.

Another type of embroidery is blackwork. Most blackwork, both historical and present day, comes from Great Britain. It was already hugely popular in the days of Henry VIII, and (although, as happens so often, experts find it difficult to agree) it was his first wife, Catherine of Aragon, who is generally credited with bringing this type of embroidery to England from her native country. The Spaniards and the Moors (who occupied large parts of Spain's territory for well over seven centuries) always were fond of rather severe, mostly geometrical, counted-thread work. In England, blackwork today is almost as popular as it was in the sixteenth century, and in North Africa, the Moroccans still make great use of it, too.

Although its outlines may be along flowing and free lines, blackwork always carries a somewhat geometrical character and is based on counting the threads of the background material. Some simple fillings using the backstitch and cross-stitch (the basis of most present-day blackwork) are shown on the opposite page. The first row consists of borders that need no further explanation. The second and third rows show just how easy it is to "play around" with one basic motif and diversify the effects of the fillings ad infinitum. The fourth row shows some examples of the kind of small motifs that can be used independently.

Audrey Morris of England sketched the design and made this delightful, modern interpretation of a bird sampler in blackwork. (The design and the embroidery were first published in *Blackwork Embroidery* by Geddes and McNeill, listed in the Bibliography.)

Outsized toy turtle with 17 different canvas stitches. Designer Charles Quaintance. (Courtesy of Alice Maynard, Inc., New York City.)

Mrs. Edith Park Martin of Katonah, New York, designed and made this abstract exercise in filling stitches. Dimensions: 10 x 12 inches, in woolen yarns on silk. (Photograph by Malcolm Varon.)

Small canvas-stitch sampler shows a highly individual approach. Worked by Julia Bullmore, Fine Art Department, Goldsmiths College, London, England.

This wall hanging has one straight-forward motif, a tree with birds, in its center. The sampler aspect came in when Mrs. Dubs, of Switzerland, surrounded it by a "frame" consisting of 372 different, tiny motifs. Each of them was worked over 12 x 18 threads of the material, and Mrs. Dubs' inspiration for these was found in old religious symbols as well as in modern traffic signs, in the alphabet as well as nature — in short, just everywhere. She openly admits that, in the process of completing this enormous project, she suffered so much mental and physical strain that, at one time, her doctor made her abandon the work for several months!

Detail shows some of the stitches used. Central design was framed by 372 small motifs in sampler by Mrs. Dubs. (Photographs courtesy of Schweizer Heimatwerk, Zurich, Switzerland.)

A very simple example of free embroidery, this "Tree of Life" pattern was done in white threads, with silver lurex details, on a very fine coral-red linen. All the leaves are exercises in stitches. This is one of the samplers I used while teaching, and the execution of the leaf fillings was left to the imagination of the pupil. Size of the panel: 9 x 12 inches.

Catherine of Aragon

Anne Boleyn

Jane Seymour

Mrs. Betty Haughey of Para Hills, South Australia, a longtime embroideress and teacher, made this extraordinary multiple sampler. King Henry VIII is surrounded by his spouses, and each panel is a technical exercise sampler: King Henry — canvas work; Catherine of Aragon — laid work; Anne Boleyn — Dorset feather stitchery; Jane Seymour — drawn fabric; Anne of Cleves — two layers of embroidered organdy, with one layer subsequently cut away from the background; Catherine Howard — blackwork; Catherine Parr — pattern darning. Size of the center panel: 14½ x 19½ inches; each of the other six panels measures 12 x 18 inches.

Anne of Cleves

Catherine Howard

Catherine Parr

Genealogical tree of the Fuerstenberg family. Dated 1604, this extraordinary embroidery presents many, often humorous, sampler characteristics, such as the strip of little pictures directly underneath the bottom row of portraits. From the collection of the Prince and Princess of Liechtenstein. (Photograph courtesy of *Plaisir de France*, Paris, France.)

Almost any design, figurative or not, can be divided into irregular shapes and used as a sampler, with the stitches worked along counted threads or in free embroidery according to the background material chosen. My "Delft Blue" sampler was done, naturally, in shades of blue, with stranded silks on heavy, white shantung. Covering some parts of such a sampler with solid stitchery, even in a free embroidery piece like this one, provides a stronger, more dramatic background for the "exercise" details.

It is rather fashionable, these days, to market embroidery kits that have part of the design preprinted in color. This, of course, greatly simplifies the work to be done and one is at liberty to either work over the preprinted parts or leave them as is.

Some of my own sampler kits were produced on this principle: the Eagle sampler shows the parts printed in red left untouched; in the Man and Wife samplers each has its printed parts outlined in the stitch shown in the drawing.

There are textile paints on the market nowadays that make it possible to execute a similar project without having to resort to a commercially produced kit. Do take care, though, to check that the label of your paint tube clearly states the paint is insoluble or washable.

Eagle sampler, worked in red, twisted cotton on white, watered silk. Size 10 x 13 inches. (First published in *House & Garden* Magazine, U.S.A., in September, 1969.)

Man and Wife samplers, one in red, the other in green, worked with stranded cotton (using three strands all the way) on white, watered silk. Size of each: 6½ x 13 inches.

Two unusual sampler figures, designed by Renee Koevoets of the Netherlands, show a great assortment of stitches on even-weave linen. These were worked along counted threads, in orange and red shades, but such figures would lend themselves equally well to an exercise in free embroidery, and many other color schemes would prove equally attractive.

Renee Koevoets is a frequent contributor to the Dutch monthly embroidery publication *Bij Voorbeeld* (*For Example*) in which these pieces were first published.

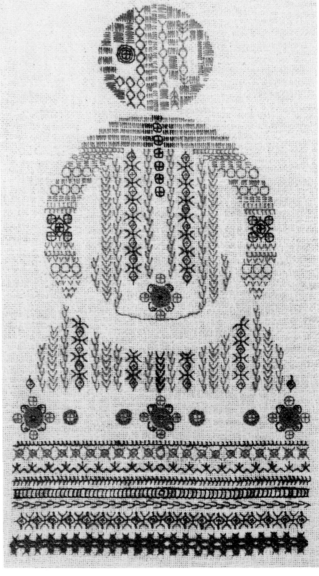

This wonderful design by Gunilla Lagerbjelke of Sweden also offers unusual possibilities for a stitch sampler. The designer made her work into a blue, red, yellow, and green, embroidered table runner, but it would be quite stupendous as the center part of a festive tablecloth. The use of just one color, or shades of one color, might emphasize the sampler character of the embroidery.

Design by Gunilla Lagerbjelke was first published in Eivor Fisher's book *Swedish Embroidery*. (Photos courtesy of B. T. Batsford, Ltd., London, England.)

Miss Kathleen Whyte of Scotland, a professional, studied the possibilities of circular shapes, using various cotton and woolen threads in this sampler, worked in white on a dark gray flannel (rather like men's suiting material). The eight circles, each about 3½ inches in diameter, are worked mainly in laid work and surface stitches.

Sampler by Kathleen Whyte, senior lecturer at the Glasgow School of Art. In the possession of the Chicago Needlework and Textile Guild, Chicago, Illinois, who kindly gave permission for reproduction.

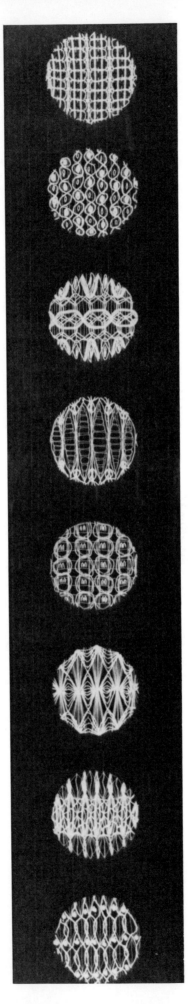

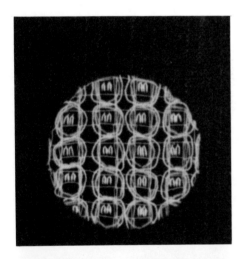

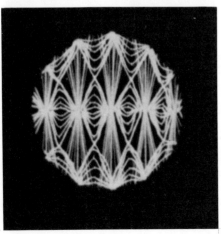

A very different use of circular shapes, executed in a completely different line of thought, is presented in a panel designed and worked by Kay Norris, a student at the Fine Art Department of London University's Goldsmiths College. She used a little appliqué and a great variety of stitches in wools and cotton to make her delightful tree. The panel was completed in 1968 and measures 6 x 8 inches.

Mrs. Harold Hughes, a teacher from North Chatham, New York, whose specialty is crewel work, made this "Apple Tree" sampler, transforming the apples into simple, very effective circular shapes.

The accent here is on the quite extraordinary variety of filling stitches shown in both the apples and the leaves, while only little space has been allotted to the basic stitch of crewel work: the long and the short stitch.

Sampler of filling stitches in circular shapes by Mrs. Harold Hughes, using scarlets and greens. Dimensions: 36 x 48 inches. (Photograph by Lees Studio.)

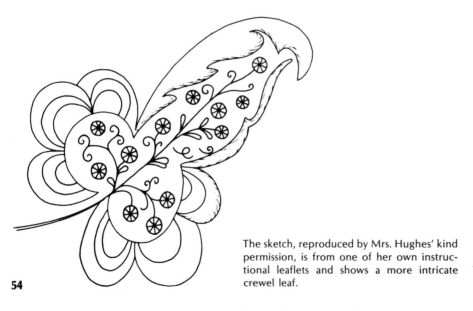

54

The sketch, reproduced by Mrs. Hughes' kind permission, is from one of her own instructional leaflets and shows a more intricate crewel leaf.

The unusual technical subject for this next sampler is quilting by hand. The sampler was executed along totally abstract, free-flowing lines in back-stitches on mauve viyella (cotton and wool mixture), with added details of herringbone and running stitches.

Kay Norris, a student at the Fine Art Department of Goldsmiths College, London University, made the sampler in 1968, using stranded cotton in mauves, blues, and purple as an embroidery thread. The size: 8 x 6½ inches.

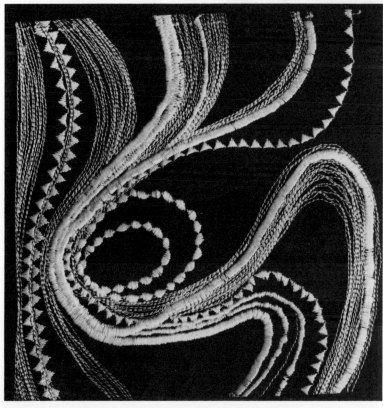

An experiment in machine stitching on black cotton cloth; executed by a pupil of the Helsinki Training College for Teachers of Handicrafts. Size approx. 6 x 8 inches. (Photo courtesy of Omin Käsin, Helsinki, Finland.)

Buttonhole stitchery, the basic stitch used in needle lace and one that was so popular in between the world wars, is not very much in fashion now. But these things have a way of coming and going, and maybe, by making buttonholing the subject of a sampler, an embroiderer might set a renewed trend for tomorrow.

Buttonhole sampler by Julia Bullmore of the Fine Art Department, Goldsmiths College, London, England. The stitches are worked partly in detached loops, partly on brass rings, and partly as a pure exercise in stitchery. Size is 6 inches in diameter. Colors: yellow merging into orange and dull pink on a natural-colored background.

Buttonhole sampler by Rebecca Crompton. (Victoria and Albert Museum, London.)

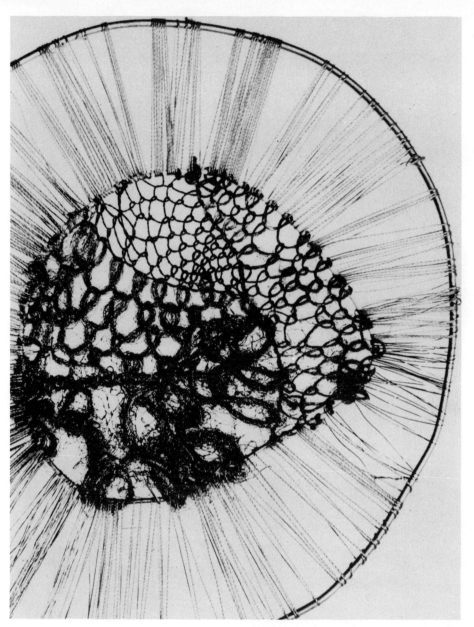

The satin stitch and couching are specialties of traditional, Japanese embroidery, which was meant to be worn and therefore consisted mainly of rather flat stitches (see color page 66). The embroidery thread used is of a rather flossy silk and it is either used singly or twisted before work, according to the effect desired.

Sometimes gold and silver details accompany the work, for which the background is again silk; at times the material has a woven pattern that bears no relationship to the embroidery.

Decorative stitchery for the home in the Western style has become increasingly popular over the last twenty-five years, and there are now a multitude of pattern books for this purpose on the Japanese market.

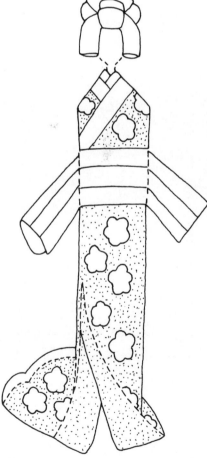

Japanese kimono of the type decorated by satin stitching and couching — based on a drawing supplied by the Ondori Publishing Co., Tokyo, Japan.

"The Four Evangelists" as worked into a sampler by Mrs. R.K. Evans of England, in the beginning of the twentieth century. Silk needle painting and couched work in gold. Size 8½ x 8½ inches. (Collection of the Embroiderers' Guild, London, England.)

Couching is very popular now in the West as well, and many artists like to experiment with new ways of exploiting this technique.

Josephine Windebank of the Fine Art Department, Goldsmiths College, London, used khaki-colored Thai silk as a background for her geometrical, couched forms in pure silk, metal threads and silk cords. Her colors are sea-blue, gold, a slightly greenish yellow and a light khaki, and the final sampler measures 9 x 9 inches.

Couched work by Josephine Windebank.

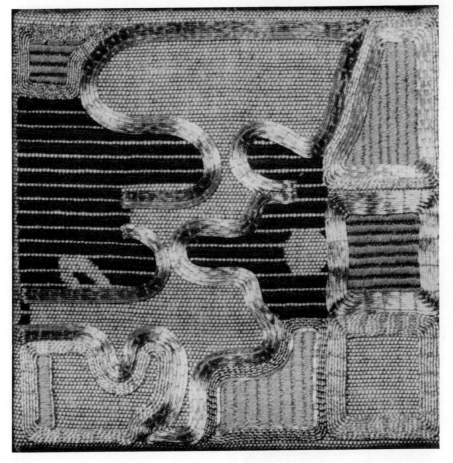

Present-day couching experiment in gold and silver threads with ochre and fawn-colored threads for the sewing down and the details of satin stitchery. Size 7 x 7 inches; by Janet Speak, pupil of the Fine Art Department, Goldsmiths College, London, England.

In her *Composition in Squares*, Mariska Karasz, the Hungarian-born artist, used a great variety of linen and cotton threads in creams, yellows, oranges, and green on an olive-colored background. The technique, once more, is mainly couching, to which a variety of needle-lace fillings were added (without, however, cutting away the background). This piece measures 65 x 52 inches.

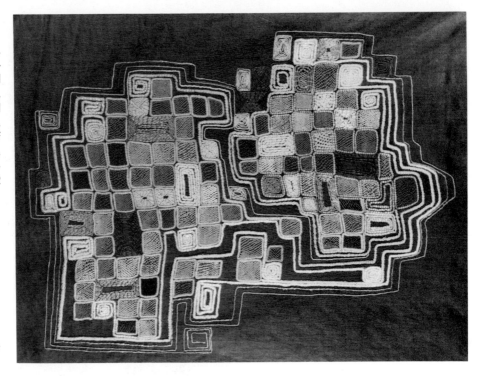

(By permission of the Cooper Union Museum, New York City.)

Karin Courtens of the Netherlands took the inspiration for her couched-work embroidery from the pattern of the material itself and made it into a robotlike figure. On the mainly mauve background, she couched silver threads into a fascinating variety of little wheels and cogs, using blue and green silks to sew the silver down. A newcomer to the field of embroidery, she also experiments with textile objects for free use in space.

The women from San'a in Yemen brought couched silver-thread work to Israel. They made a series of samplers of their traditional embroideries for the Israel Museum in Jerusalem. There, a Jewish bride can be seen wearing such decorations on the leggings of her gorgeous wedding-day costume. The Yemen embroideries have also been adapted for modern-day wear and have even become part of Israel's folk-art export.

(Courtesy of the Israel Museum, Jerusalem, Israel; David Harris, photographer.)

(Courtesy of the Israel Museum.)

The everyday leggings of Muslim and of Jewish women from San'a, Yemen, were of a completely different type. All the rows but the top one of the embroidery sampler shown on this page are executed in chain-stitch variations such as those worn by the Jewish women, while the cross-stitch row at the top is of a type used in the villages by Muslims.

The colors on the sampler are traditional, mainly red stitches on black cloth, with details in white and green. Here again, the technique has been adapted to modern life and has become part of Israel's folklore, as the apparel of the young Israeli dancers shown here demonstrates. The Yemenite embroideries of today, attractive as they are, should not, however, be too closely compared to the fabulous quality of some of the old pieces.

Sampler of everyday wear embroidery for leggings, Yemenite. (Photo courtesy of the Israel Museum, Jerusalem.)

Detail of modern Yemenite embroidery from Israel. (Author's collection.)

Young Israeli folk dancers. The embroidery on their clothes is directly inspired by Yemenite sources. (Author's collection.)

Moroccan embroidery, as it stands today, is mainly based upon old motifs, brought back to Morocco around the year 1600 when Philip III finally expelled the Moors from his country (large parts of Spain having been occupied by the Moors from the early part of the eighth century).

In accordance with Muslim traditions, most Moroccan embroidery represents no living being, but concentrates on stylized floral forms, often transformed into geometrical shapes.

Sampler in silk on cotton, nineteenth-century Fès. (Photograph courtesy of the Victoria and Albert Museum, London, England.)

Much embroidery is still being done in Morocco both by amateurs and professional embroideresses, partly for the tourist trade. The majority of the work still is identical on both sides of the material; this stems from the fact that Moroccan embroideries were always meant for use and not for wall decorations.

Moroccan women have great instinct and feeling for fine work, but none at all for the quality of materials used. Incredibly delicate, counted-thread work in silks may be executed on a completely inferior quality of cotton background. Sometimes the pieces of cotton underneath the work have even been sewn together by machine, using up bits of background material left over from previous projects.

Furthermore, as the needleworkers are paid by the weight of the silk used in their embroidery, there is (with the increasing tourist market) a strong tendency towards very thick, ungainly work, using as much silk as will possibly pass through the material at one time for every single stitch. Nevertheless, the embroideries of Rabat, Salé, Fès and Meknès still represent a very distinct, personal character, well worth exploring.

Moroccan work is often executed on the bias, starting from the bottom left and going towards the top right, and then returning in a technique resembling the Holbein stitch. The designs in the drawing were taken from Fès and Meknès embroideries.

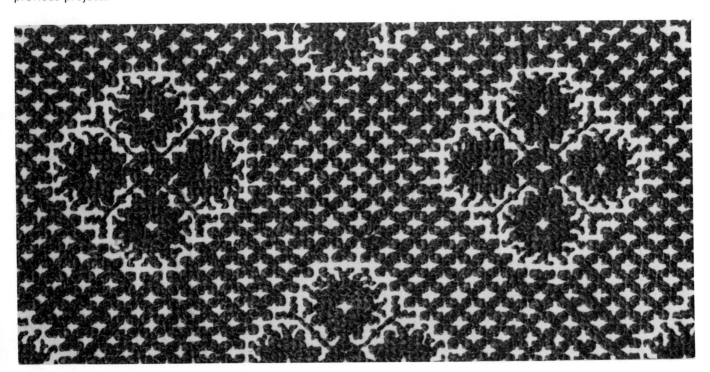

Detail of twentieth-century Fès embroidery in black silk on unbleached cotton. (Author's collection.)

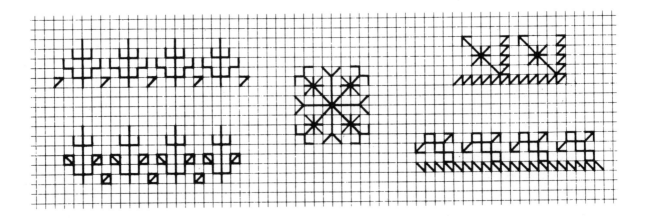

64

The common sources of Moroccan and Spanish embroideries are clearly visible in the beautiful, severe, typically Spanish sampler shown here. Although it dates from 1756, it might inspire any present-day needleworker with a taste for understatement and the nerve for a time-consuming project.

Spanish sampler, 1756, silks and drawn-thread work on linen. (Photograph courtesy of the Victoria and Albert Museum, London, England.)

Samplers of traditional Japanese silk embroideries, as used on kimonos and the accompanying obis (intricately draped strips of silk worn around the waist). (Photographs courtesy of the Ondori Publishing Company, Tokyo, Japan.)

One end and detail of a Rooshnick, by Mrs. Anna Wyshivala. (Courtesy of the Ukrainian National Women's League of America, Philadelphia, Pennsylvania.)

Spanish influences spread to Mexico, too, but the motifs gradually softened and only the white, drawn-thread work remained closely reminiscent of its ancestors. Mexican samplers, like Moroccan embroideries, often have a background that has previously been put together out of remnants of material and then embroidered. Worn mostly on regional costumes today, the embroidery in some regions is worked on separate bands, all with different motifs, and sewn together afterward as a bodice, the bands forming a sampler in their own right.

Detail of present-day blouse from Puebla, Mexico, showing true sampler characteristics. (Author's collection.)

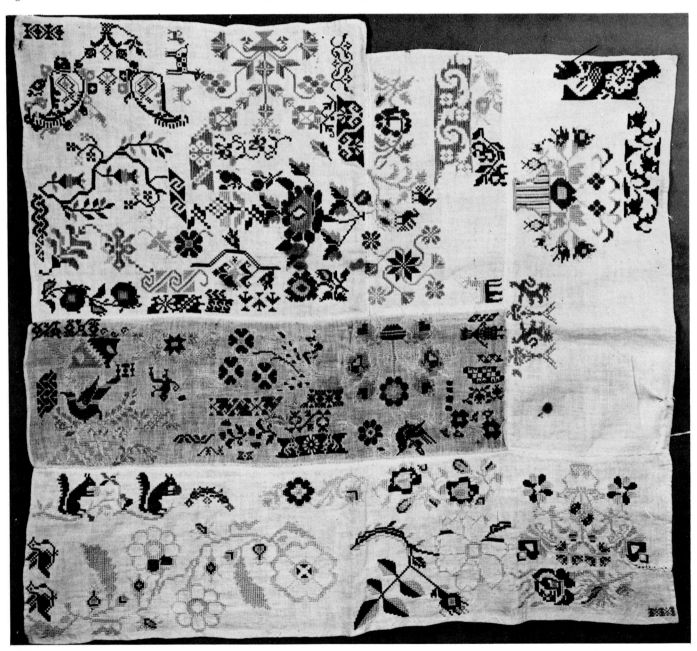

Mexican sampler, circa 1900. The embroidery is clearly overlapping the seams of the pieced background in some places. (Photograph courtesy of Museo Nacional de Antropologia, Mexico City, D.F., Mexico.)

Differing from Moroccan and Spanish embroidery, Turkish embroidery has its own special characteristics. Although much beautiful embroidery is being done in Turkey today, sampler making has little part in it. The reason for this lies mainly in the extremely elaborate, painted design from which the work is copied; this leaves little or nothing to the worker's own initiative or imagination. Not only all colors, but also the direction of the stitches, are already worked out on the "master design."

Turkish drawing. Author's collection. (Photograph by Mort Kaye.)

Another region that has long been famous for its extremely beautiful, and very typical, embroideries is the Ukraine. There is an active Ukrainian National Women's League in the United States, and most of the members embroider. Apart from making technical samplers, such as those used as a practical guide for work typical of their country of origin, the Ukrainian women make a kind of picture sampler that bears the name of "Rooshnick."

A Rooshnick — a long cloth, usually measuring about 18 x 48 inches, and embroidered on both ends in a variety of stitches — is by tradition considered to be a symbol of protection against evil, as well as a token of high esteem and goodwill. Ukrainian women drape these embroideries around the icons in their homes. (See color pictures on page 67.)

Technical sampler of stitches used in Ukrainian embroidery, by Mrs. Tania Diakin O'Neill.

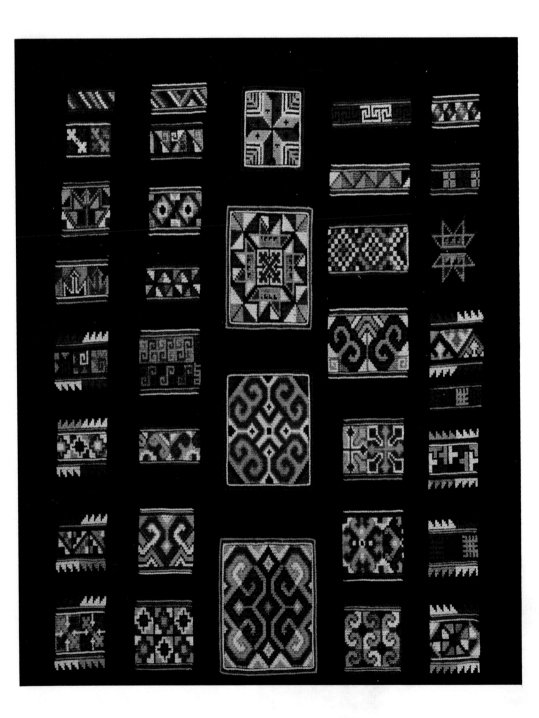

These samplers present all the traditional, symbolic storytelling patterns used by Yao women in Thailand. The embroideries were obtained through the courtesy of Miss Jacqueline Butler. (Photographs by Malcolm Varon.)

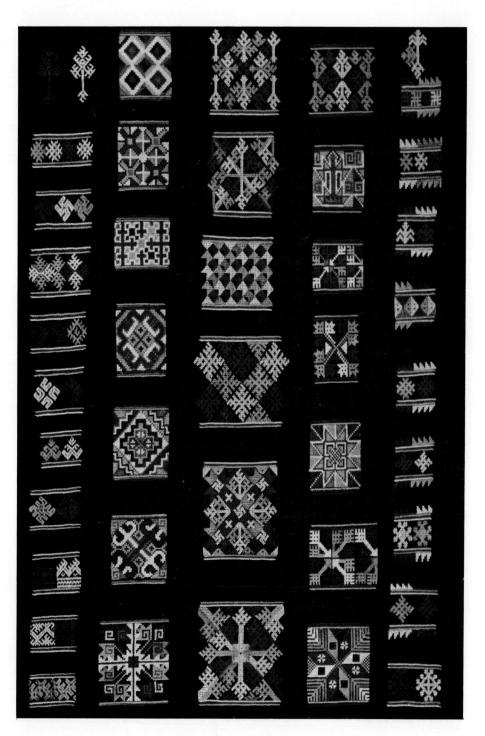

Storytelling Samplers

In Thailand, women of the Yao hill tribe embroider storytelling samplers on the baggy trousers that form part of their traditional costume. Each girl chooses ten out of the over sixty existing Yao patterns (each has a very specific, symbolic meaning) and, in embroidering her chosen designs, she makes a statement regarding her own qualities and creative abilities. This becomes an important factor in attracting a future husband.

"To a Yao man, the precision, quality and colors of these embroideries are deciding factors in a girl's marriageability," writes Miss Jacqueline Butler, who lived and worked in Thailand for two years and spent her spare time researching this subject.

She adds: "A Yao girl learns the traditional embroidery patterns when she is five or six years old and begins working on her trousers soon afterward, sometimes adding new designs and color inventions of her own, so that the Yao art, although traditional, yet remains constantly alive and changing."

Storytelling samplers par excellence, the Yao patterns are embroidered statements on love, nature, the spiritual world, legends, and daily life. The patterns all carry names, such as: "Celestial Crown," "Encircling Claws," "Big Flower Tail," "Tiger Ear" and "Hunter's Blind."

Technically the work consists of straight stitches and diagonal or horizontal cross-stitches, all embroidery being done from the back of the cloth.

One leg of a Yao woman's trousers (both legs are identical). Detail shows straight stitches and cross-stitches. (Photographs by Malcolm Varon.)

Yao women at work. In the villages, they will gather and work in groups, chatting incessantly (one thinks of quilting bees). They are perhaps the only women in the world to have given a name, "Manq Zor," to their all-consuming hobby; this expression means, "being crazy about needlework."

These are details of storytelling samplers shown in color on pages 70 and 71. The samplers were made by Yao women especially for Miss Jacqueline Butler of Tempe, Arizona, who worked in Thailand for two years and has written a locally produced book on this fascinating aspect of folk art. (Photographs by Malcolm Varon.)

Although beadwork is a technique that is not often incorporated in Western samplers these days, quite extraordinary and unusual pictorial effects can be obtained, as illustrated by the delightful beadwork sampler made on linen by Virginia Capparucci in nineteenth-century Italy.

Mexico is another country where beadwork has always been much beloved. Curious triangular, knotted ends of a cloth from Monterey, Nuevo Leon, have beaded patterns incorporated into them; each triangle (about 2 x 2 to 3 x 3 inches at its widest) tells a different story of the husband, the wife, and of what presumably represents their cattle, domesticated animals, and other assets.

Beadwork sampler. (Courtesy of the Metropolitan Museum of Art, New York City, Collection of Mrs. Lathrop Colgate Harper, bequest, 1957.)

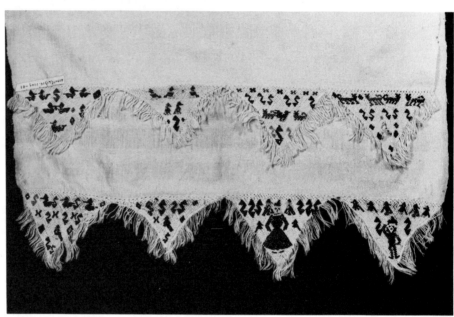

Mexican beadwork. (Courtesy of the Museo Nacional de Antropologia, Mexico City, D.F., Mexico.)

Beaded Zulu panel. (Author's collection.)

In South Africa, the Zulu girl wears a series of tiny beadwork samplers as love letters around her throat. All her hopes and disappointments are written down in this way, each pattern and each color having its own significance. An all-white panel without decoration may mean faithfulness to one who is absent; red will indicate jealousy; black the longing for marriage. An entire language is spoken in beads by the extremely code-and-symbol conscious Zulus, and the young girl's love letters are part of a quite complex indication system that tells of Zulu marriage, virtue, riches, and many other life aspects.

Lately, the Zulus have also engaged in the making of small storytelling beaded panels such as the one shown here, which is worked in vivid reds, greens, blues, white and black.

In our own Western countries, story-telling samplers have also, at times, taken on unusual contexts. Around the year 1800, for example, a great taste for melancholy developed, and it rapidly became the fashion to make elaborate "mourning" pictures. These represented graves and urns, and the grieving embroideress was often present, clutching a handkerchief, under a tree with sadly hanging branches. If at all possible, some of both the mourner's and the dear departed's hair was added to the embroidery as a final, delicate touch. In samplers of that period, tombstones, urns, and mausoleums often figured prominently.

French sampler, late eighteenth-century, silk on silk in free embroidery, with the addition of silver and gold thread and sequins. At the bottom, a variety of mourning patterns. (Courtesy of the Victoria and Albert Museum, London, England.)

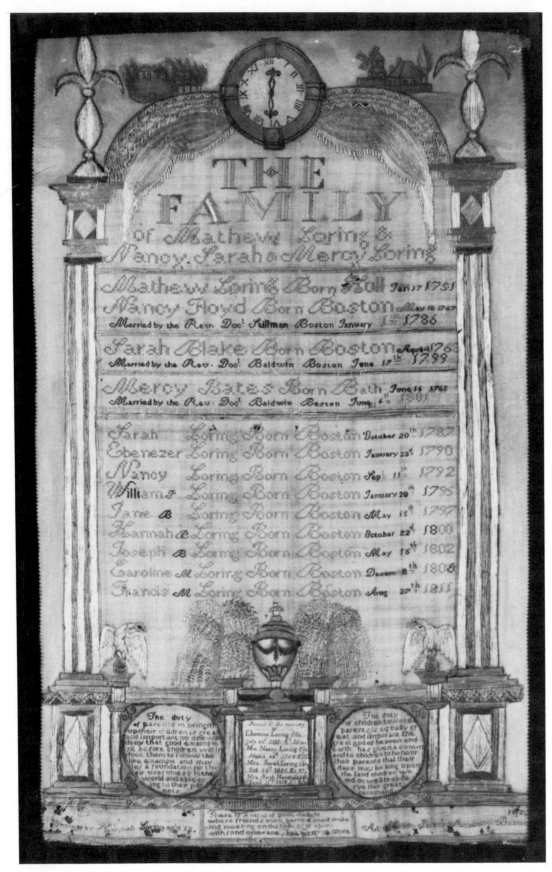

Sampler of the Loring family, 1812, by Hannah
Loring, in silk on linen. (Courtesy of the
Metropolitan Museum of Art, New York City,
bequest of Mabel Herbert Harper, 1957.)

Embroidered mosque by Kay Norris, Fine Art Department, Goldsmiths College, London, England, 1967.

To get back to less morose subjects, in many twentieth-century samplers, buildings of some description are used to contain exercises in stitchery. The mosque sampler, by Kay Norris of England, is an exercise in couched work in mauves, purples, and pinks on a coarse linen background, using soft cotton as embroidery thread.

A patient at the Metropolitan Hospital in New York City embroidered this touching story, of the view from her window, on a small panel covered with cotton thread in an infinite variety of stitches and colors.

Picture sampler, 1948. (Courtesy of the Cooper-Hewitt Museum of Design, New York City.)

The next two samplers resulted from a very special project undertaken by the Northwest Branch of the London Embroiderers' Guild, when the Guild moved to Wimpole Street in 1961. Six members embroidered samplers depicting the facade of the new headquarters; each sampler measured 13½ x 5½ inches, and each one was worked in a different technique. The samplers were subsequently mounted into a small, decorative screen that now forms part of the Guild's embroidery collection. Two of the six panels are represented here — one done in blackwork, which is still so very popular with the English; the other in creamy-colored even-weave linen with pulled work, drawn-thread work and a variety of simple stitches.

An interesting contrast between these two samplers has resulted from the fact that in the second panel the windows were emphasized, while in the blackwork piece the front itself was given prime emphasis.

The same subject was embroidered in blackwork and also in pulled work, drawn-thread work, and other stitches. (Both photographs courtesy of The Embroiderers' Guild, London, England.)

Similarly, almost any house might be translated into a sampler embroidery, by simply copying the main outlines of a good, enlarged photograph and taking it from there.

However wild and modernistic its air, the patchwork piece featuring embroidered buildings dates from the second half of the nineteenth century! It is attributed to Celestine Bacheller of Wyoma, Massachusetts. Crazy patchwork quilts were quite a fad for a while, and this lady certainly let herself go when she put together the myriad pieces that compose the re-embroidered bedquilt, of which only part is shown here.

Detail of patchwork quilt, late nineteenth-century. (Courtesy of the Museum of Fine Arts, Boston, Massachusetts.)

An extraordinary sampler, worked in silks on linen, was made by one Laura Hyde in the year 1800. It also is curiously modern and very clever in concept: the different parts of the Indian City, the boats floating in the Bay of Bengal and a view of the local grandee's harem flow effortlessly into the parts that carry the text and emblems. Describing a harem scene, the text tells of the presence of the British Ambassador's wife during a visit to the women's quarters, and one wonders whether the American, who made the sampler, was in her company or perhaps belonged to the harem itself.

Not an easy project to design, this type of sampler work would need very careful planning.

American sampler, 1800, silk on linen. (Courtesy of the Metropolitan Museum of Art, New York City, Rogers Fund, 1944.)

In many countries, women delight in telling the stories of birth, a life, a marriage, a house — embroidering mainly cross-stitch patterns on a sampler that can be read like a book. My country-women are amongst these and, in their handiwork, every little motif has a very definite meaning. The coat of arms of the town or country that sets the scene for the sampler, the number of children, the life style, hobbies and activities of the family, their religion — all these and many more details about either the maker of the sampler or the person for whom it was made can be learned from perusing such a piece.

Events are related with appropriate motifs. In this sampler by Mrs. van Kinschot-Dorhout Mees, for example, the birth of a grandchild in Ethiopia is designated by that country's symbol.

Certainly intricate, and worked with love and patience, is this magnificent sampler by Mrs. Nijpels-Kamerlingh Onnes. It measures approximately 20 x 16 inches and is worked in silks on linen.

Mrs. Goedkoop-Würdemann commemorated the birth of each of her children with a separate sampler. Her samplers are all worked in several shades of one color only, producing a quite unusual effect.

One of Mrs. Braat-Bertel's children married and went to live in South Africa. Motifs in the sampler relate to the couple's Dutch ancestry, their honeymoon travels and their South African residence.

A beautiful, early Colonial-style mansion forms the centerpiece of this sampler from Tasmania (Australia). Mrs. May Scott used an abundance of stitches to depict her home, "Woodside," which has housed five generations of the Scott family, and she added the lovely old trees and shrubs which surround the house. The sampler, in various colors on finely woven, cream linen, is dated 1969.

A Danish house, in another sampler, is also surrounded by local flora and fauna. The work is done in the typically Danish, fine cross-stitch work and is surrounded by a very effective, very twentieth-century border. It is reproduced here by kind permission of the Haandarbejdets Fremme organization in Copenhagen, Denmark, whose property this joyous sampler is.

(Photo courtesy of Selskabet til Haandarbejdets Fremme, Copenhagen, Denmark.)

A 1970 storytelling sampler from Australia has a fascinating, family story to it. In 1914, one Albert Mead Richardson enlisted in the Australian Infantry. While on leave in England, he met and fell in love with Mable Annie Swinburne. In the conventional manner of those times, he did not drag her off to his country when the war was over, but just went back alone to build a house and prepare a farm, before he let his bride-to-be come out.

The sampler was made by one of the Richardson's daughters, Mrs. Margaret Siddall, on the occasion of the couple's fiftieth wedding anniversary. It tells the whole story of their hardworking life and the capers of their children. At the bottom, left and right, the parents' hobbies are shown: Mr. Richardson is a watercolor painter in his spare time and occasionally has one-man shows; his wife loves to sit outside and feed the birds.

Mrs. Siddall worked her panel in a classical manner, using fine cross-stitches in natural colors; the finished size is approximately 10 x 15 inches. Her husband and her son collaborated in most of the designing and therefore she included their initials in small backstitch lettering (bottom left-hand corner).

A Danish embroidery, called "Sampler of the Queen," is dedicated to the present Queen Mother, wife of the late King Frederick IX and formerly Princess of Sweden. It depicts the palaces of the Danish Royal Family and their coats of arms. The birthdates of the King and Queen's three daughters (the oldest of whom is the present Queen Margrethe) figure amongst a host of smaller details.

Such commemorative pieces were popular in England in Queen Victoria's time and they still make their appearance occasionally in countries with a Royal Family to boast of.

In the Netherlands, a commemorative sampler was published in the women's magazine *Margriet* in honor of Crown Princess Beatrix. It was subsequently copied by hundreds of Dutch housewives and given a place of honor in their homes. The Crown Princess herself received several dozen of them as a wedding present.

Commemorative sampler for the Royal Danish family was designed by Gerda Bengtsson. (Photograph courtesy Selskabet til Haandarbejdets Fremme, Copenhagen, Denmark.)

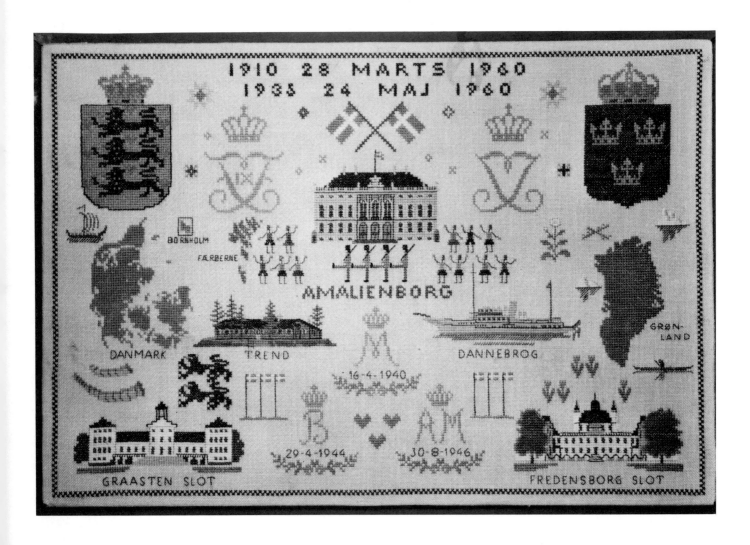

1950 ✦ 1954

Sampler by Mrs. G.S. Fletcher. (Photograph courtesy of the Embroiderers' Guild, London, England.)

An extremely intricate sampler-picture of a house is "The Spirit of Cape Colony" (above). It took the maker, Mrs. G.S. Fletcher of South Africa, four years to complete, and it won first prize at an international exhibition organized by the English Embroiderers' Guild (London, 1955). The sampler depicts life in the eighteenth century at the Cape Colony. Especially fascinating are the details of ostriches at the bottom, and at the right the three Kaffirs carrying fruits and vegetables, with a bird about to nibble at the delicacies.

The two entrance doors, open at the bottom left and right, are incredible in their well-balanced, yet so distinctive, detail.

A curious mixture of many story-telling elements is this patchwork quilt — not the story of a family but of a country. The Turks are shown invading Austria; Death menacingly holds his scythe among some tombstones. The city is embattled. There are a host of small surrounding panels showing, nostalgically, the former daily life of peace, love, music, and art.

Historical storytelling sampler from Prague, 1790. (Photograph courtesy of the Victoria and Albert Museum, London, England.)

A most unusual family sampler was embroidered on the front of a christening dress by Mrs. Susi Katz of Switzerland. She made the dress (below) not only for her own children, but also for close members of her family so that subsequently the names of Swiss-, Dutch- and Peruvian-born babies were added to the family baptismal dress. These names and dates surround beautifully worked symbolical motifs, which relate to religion and fecundity.

Mrs. Katz delights in the working of feathered animals that, under her able hands, become stitch samplers in their own right. Shown at the right are three details from Mrs. Katz's embroidered, white linen tablecloth, which she calls, "My Chicken Family." (Photos courtesy of Schweizer Heimatwerk, Zurich.)

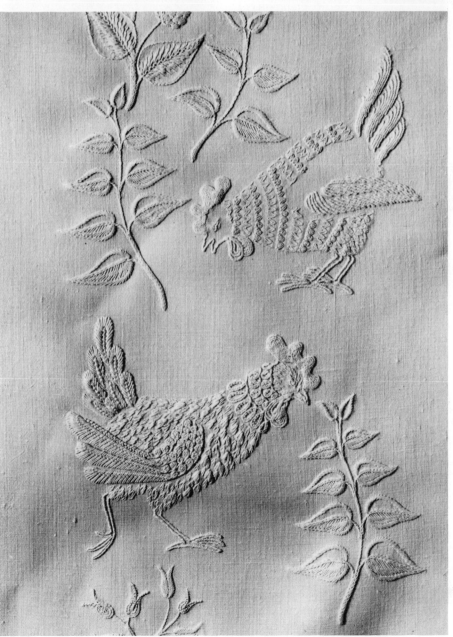

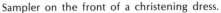
Sampler on the front of a christening dress.

A fabulous storytelling sampler from Germany was stitched by Mrs. Sigrid Teske. Her story starts in 1942, when she married, and the bottom part of the sampler shows her husband and herself symbolically planting the tree of their life together. As the tree grows, children's names are added on the left side, the dates of birth on the right.

Countless details accompany the growing tree: the couple's new start in life after World War II was over, their life together in the countryside, the arrival of eight children — amongst them twin boys, the death of one small baby, all the joys and sorrows of daily life. At the top of the tree, there is a picture of the whole family, the children growing up and taking over some of the tasks of their parents.

The delicacy of this silk embroidery is incredible; just look at the rich fantasy that went into the making of so many different trees, the loving care with which each detail is brought to life. And all this is the work of a housewife leading the simplest of hardworking lives, with no artistic or technical training whatsoever. Mrs. Teske never studied embroidery or drawing and had no more help other than what she read in the Swiss publication *Heimatwerk* and an occasional encouraging letter from its editors. The time to do embroidery was found as the elder children grew up and, by doing her baking for her and by occasionally looking after the small fry, they enabled her to spend most of her evenings and Sundays on this entirely lovable piece of work (and many others of the same quality).

Storytelling sampler and detail by Mrs. Sigrid Teske. (Photos courtesy of Schweizer Heimatwerk, Zurich, Switzerland.)

An interesting "written" family tree was made by Mabel Savile-von Bothmer in 1933. On the left, the names of the husband's family (Earls of Mexborough) and their motto "Be Fast." On the right, those of her own family (Counts von Bothmer) and their motto: "Respice Finem." The lettering is surrounded by considerable detail pertaining to the private life of the Savile-von Bothmer family and there is a traditional flower border around the entire sampler. The size is approximately 11 x 21 inches; done in cross and half cross-stitch, and backstitch.

A family history sampler by Mabel Savile-von Bothmer. (Photo courtesy Mrs. V. de Bruijn van Gouderack-Savile, daughter of the maker, in whose possession the sampler is.)

91

Mrs. Helen Cunningham of Winnipeg, Canada, has been living with her husband in the Colonial-style home shown near the text of her sampler for well over twenty years. A few years ago, she visited Great Britain in search of her and her husband's family histories and found out that both families had been farmers for many generations. Hence the title "Farmer's Arms" and the proud text that begins, "Let the Wealthy and Great/Roll in Splendour and State/I envy them not." She also included a shamrock for the Irish Cunninghams and a spray of heather for the Scotch Ronalds (her own name).

The size of the sampler, which includes a host of other family-connected data as well as an alphabet and ciphering, is 17 x 23 inches. It is worked entirely in fresh, natural colors on Danish cross-stitch canvas with two threads of stranded cotton.

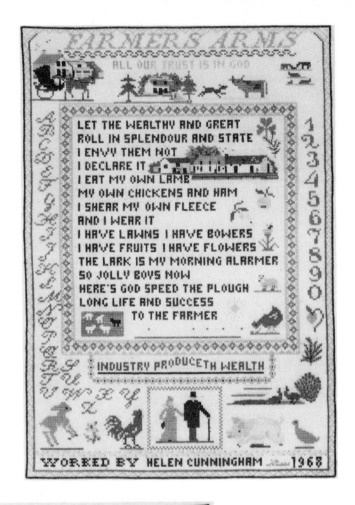

Worked in the Danish, delicate cross-stitch manner, this tree of life at the left is a genealogical one at the same time, its many branches surrounded by 200 years of family history. The names and dates are worked in backstitch. This is a project that would be easily adaptable to the needs of anyone with a yen for this type of sampler.

Danish tree of life sampler. (Photo courtesy of the Selskabet til Haandarbejdets Fremme, Copenhagen Denmark.)

Miss Mary Johnson of Kent, Connecticut, took up crewel work and embroidery at the age of 76, under the expert guidance of Mrs. Doris Thacher. Some twelve years later, she is still an ardent crewel worker. In the Grandma Moses-style sampler at the right, measuring 14 x 15 inches, she not only depicts her cat and her dog but also uses animal and insect motifs to symbolize some of her friends. Heading the exercises in stitchery is the motto: "Never explain, never complain."

Instead of incorporating diverse biographical information, some storytelling samplers emphasize one specific, personal interest. Such hobby samplers range from a simple, straightforward enterprise, well within the reach of the average embroideress, to highly individual expressions of sophisticated workmanship.

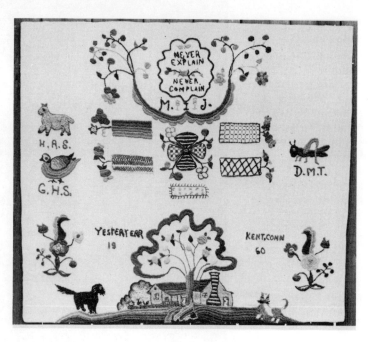

The small, very much to the point, cross-stitch sampler shown here was made in 1958, by my dear friend, the late Asta Hauch-Holm. Danish-born, she spent most of her life in England and was a perfectionist in needlework. This visual expression of her passion for embroidery measures only 9 x 9½ inches and is done in pastel shades of stranded cotton on natural-colored even-weave linen. The two big initials within the flowered wreath are those of her children. Spinning wheel, loom, tatting spool and bobbin-lace shuttle, needle, thread, thimble, scissors and a sewing machine — the whole world of textiles is represented in simple cross-stitches and backstitches. There is no attempt at intricate, ornate effects and in that lies the work's particular charm.

A music lover's sampler worked in the form of a bellpull is traditional in character if not in shape; the motifs could be adapted to many different sizes. Enormously popular, these designs are widely marketed and come in kits together with all materials. The patterns are not painted on the background material; they have to be counted from separate printed patterns included in the kits. A detail of one motif shows the extremely fine cross-stitches. These examples were worked on fine even-weave linen.

Bellpull sampler with musical motifs, designed by Clara Waever, Denmark. Fine even-weave linen with various colored cottons. Cross-stitch and backstitch. (Photograph by Koefoed; photograph of detail by Mort Kaye.)

Done in half cross-stitch on canvas, a different hobby sampler was created by the wife of Brig. General Theodore Roosevelt, Jr., to reflect his interest in wild life. Her husband, like his famous father, President Theodore Roosevelt, was an ardent hunter.

The framed size of the sampler is 22 x 15½ inches and the embroidery was done according to the animals' natural colors. The piece was very kindly put at my disposal by the embroideress's daughter-in-law, Mrs. Theodore Roosevelt III, in whose possession it now is.

An enchantingly primitive animal sampler from Mexico was worked in multi-colored cross-stitches, with cotton, on a very unusual background: the cloth was woven on a back-strap loom using henequen fiber and is light brown, almost tan, in color. The piece is of Maya origin and is part of Mrs. Irmgard Johnson's collection. An expert on Mexican textiles, Mrs. Johnson acquired the sampler in Mérida, Yucatan, and states it is definitely not more than twenty-five years old.

The interests of many Swiss embroideresses, who live in the country, are very much tied in with rural matters. Mrs. Erika Boeniger made this enchanting wall hanging, a picture sampler of all the fowl of her childhood county of Tessin. Even her two little daughters are represented as two small busy hens (top left corner) whose respective ages can be determined by the number of eggs at the right side of the embroidery. Interesting details are also found in the trail of hens' feet, at the lower right. Each of the tracks has been transformed by subtle stitchery into a tiny bug, butterfly, spiderweb or flower.

The rooster appears self-assured in his kingdom, and a large peacock, carrying his splendid train of feathers with infinite disdain, is about to wander off the material. All of the background is covered with stitchery, in different color shades and directions, and gives the piece a crazy-quilt air. The variety of stitches used in this very personal, strong piece of work is quite enormous, bringing it well within the realm of technical samplers, though it is an utterly delightful hobby and storytelling sampler as well.

Embroidered fowl. (Photo courtesy of Schweizer Heimatwerk, Zurich, Switzerland.)

Insects are the embroidery love of Mrs. Hanni Michel of Switzerland, who charted an incredible variety of them right down the middle of a fabulous housecoat. The insects all seem to be very much alive and preoccupied with their daily chores as they parade up the silk strip. The embroidery is in stranded silks and the background emphasizes the insect shapes through delicate, very cleverly directed, flat stitches in a golden color.

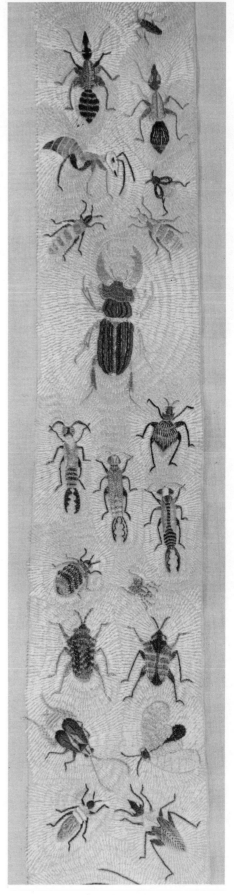

Embroidered insects. (Photos courtesy of Schweizer Heimatwerk, Zurich, Switzerland.)

A very different kind of hobby is shown by this sampler in which the patterns are based on Mexican motifs found in the British Museum. The designs are executed in couched gold and silver threads on a background of black velvet, incorporating a multitude of different wristwatch parts.

The maker of this very much out-of-the-ordinary piece of work is Susan Gaskell, a student of Miss Constance Howard's at London's Goldsmiths College. She completed the 15 x 9 inch piece in 1970.

Mrs. J.R. Carter of Midland, Texas, incorporates mounted insects in her embroideries, which have been successfully exhibited at Dallas' famous Neiman Marcus department store. This embroidery, showing a great variety of butterflies, is called, "What Is So Rare as a Day in June ?"

Very often, modern embroideresses like to base their sampler design on an especially favored old love, adapting it and translating it into twentieth-century "language." A typical example of this is the work of Mrs. Schoone-Slop of Holland shown on color page 122. She took the beautiful seventeenth-century sampler-style shown here as a starting point, embroidering the stitch exercises in the left-hand border and embroidering a very typical text *around* the various other motifs; yet her work is very much of our present time. Not only a perfectionist embroideress was at work here, but also one with a very personal, original approach to composition.

Dutch sampler combining technical exercises with written text and an intricate variety of sampler motifs. Date 1663. (Courtesy of Het Nederlands Openluchtmuseum, Arnhem, the Netherlands.)

Samplers combining a story and a technical exercise are somewhat rare but by no means new. At times, such an embroidery may incorporate the stitches into the forms that tell the story; more often, the two sampler types are simply combined on one piece of material. An example of the latter technique is this disarming, nineteenth-century Italian sampler, which might have been made yesterday. The maker, Maria Moratti, shows herself in the garden apparently about to sit down and start the stitch exercises depicted over her head, or the accompanying text at the bottom, which reads: "Man must love God above all, and his fellow man like himself."

Embroidered mottoes of all sorts are often collected as part of general sampler history. A present-day motto sampler worked by Mrs. B.G. Woodham of McColl, South Carolina, emphasizes her hobby. She embroidered the work in green, on natural-colored linen, using cross- and stem stitches (1966).

Apart from embroidering old texts, it might be amusing to work one's own family motto, or a self-composed verse, and surround the words with suitable symbols.

100

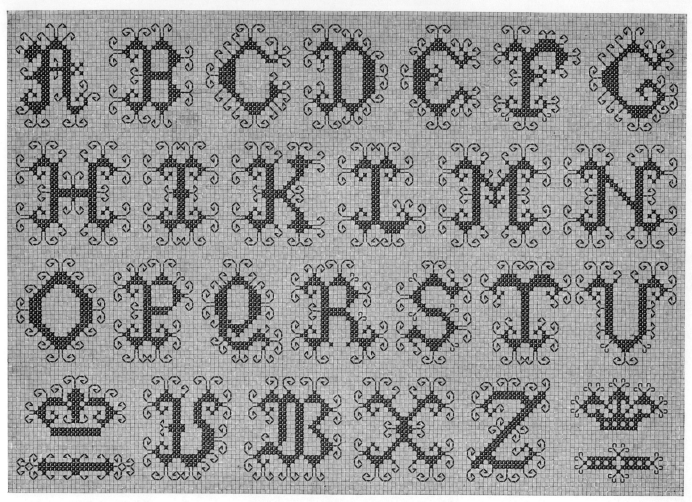

An old counted-thread alphabet.

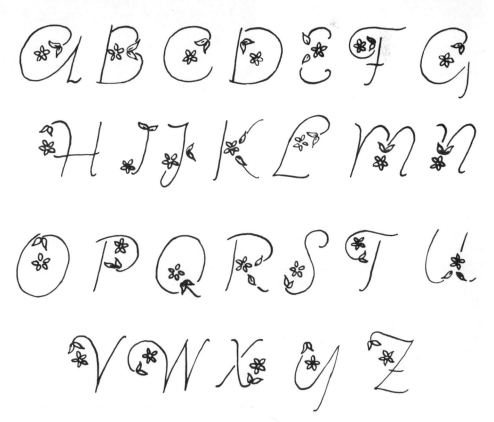

A modern free-embroidery alphabet.

The Alphabet

The alphabet has been an important part of sampler work ever since the sixteenth-century, when riches started to spread in our Western countries and the need for marking personal possessions began to be felt. Although today we no longer resort to embroidery for this purpose, the joy of playing with alphabets and numbers has remained alive with many needleworkers. Amongst them is Miss Pat Russell, who recently wrote a fascinating book on the subject.

Her alphabet is an exercise in machine embroidery and has been done not only with great dexterity and inventiveness, but also with a great deal of manifest enjoyment. She used white threads on black felt.

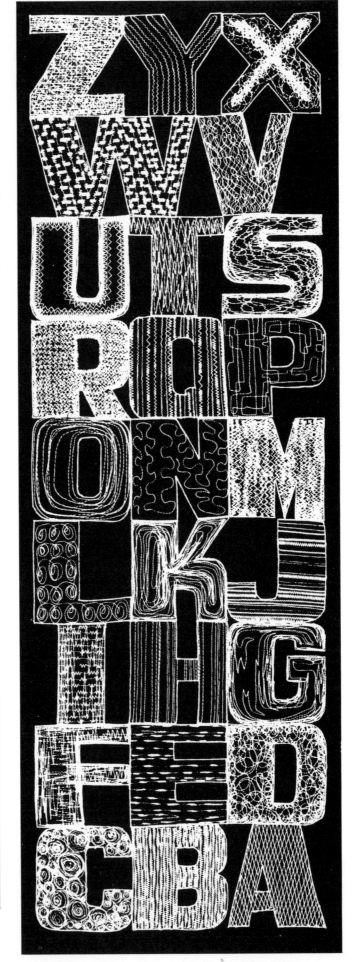

Janet Speak, a student at the Fine Art Department of London University's Goldsmiths College, made a very striking sampler experiment based exclusively on the letter "A." She made use of leather and cloth appliqué, couching, and straight stitches in stranded cottons, on a plain calico background. The finished piece measures 12 square inches; the colors used are blacks, browns, grays, and a dull red.

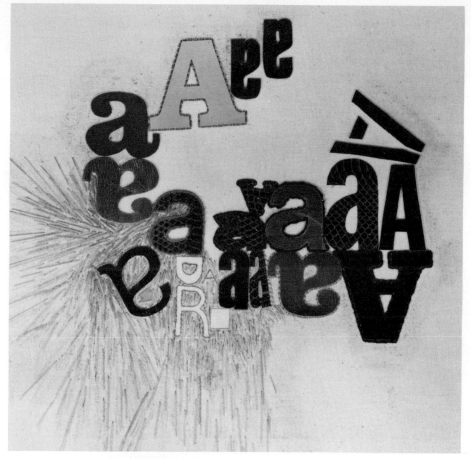

In another experiment, Janet began with a panel of unbleached cotton and dyed some areas red and green. Then she couched twisted-and-stranded cottons to outline the undyed parts in reds, greens, and browns. Although the 14 x 10 inch panel appears to be done in appliqué, no applied work of any description was used in it.

A delightful animal alphabet, done in Danish cross-stitch, shows contrasting aspects of the animal kingdom. The panel has doves next to a bear, a donkey looking around at a snake, and a fish chasing a not overly worried tiger. The letters are done in red and each carries a small, accompanying symbol, such as the delightful little moon worked close to the capital letter M and the sun next to the letter S. For the rest, natural colors are used.

The "Wildflower Alphabet" sampler is an American production. It is worked on cream linen in natural colors and measures 17 x 23½ inches.   Especially attractive is the division of the panel into irregular spaces, which takes away all possible monotony and makes the whole piece look light, fresh and airy, although it contains a considerable amount of lettering and patterns.

Danish animal alphabet by Mads Stage. (Photo by Koefoed, courtesy of Clara Waever, Copenhagen, Denmark.)

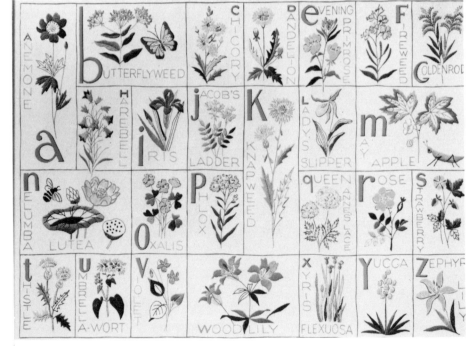

Wildflower alphabet sampler. (Photo courtesy of Paragon Needlecraft, New York City.)

The preoccupation with lettering for samplers has, at times, been quite formidable. Many historical samplers were exercises in different kinds of stitches, shapes, and sizes for the letters of the alphabet alone, and excluded any other motif. Other alphabet exercises were transformed into a combination of lettering and text as the centerpiece of a sampler, with the surrounding embroidery serving as a frame only. Present-day experimenters interested in alphabets can find much — and often unexpected — inspiration in old sampler books or lettering books.

Detail of a lettering sampler (in shaded colors) made in a Dutch orphanage, 1893. (Author's collection.) Old orphanage samplers often present a very distinct character; every square inch of the material at hand had to be exploited, so that the orphanage samplers are amongst the most minutely worked and most intricate ones every produced.

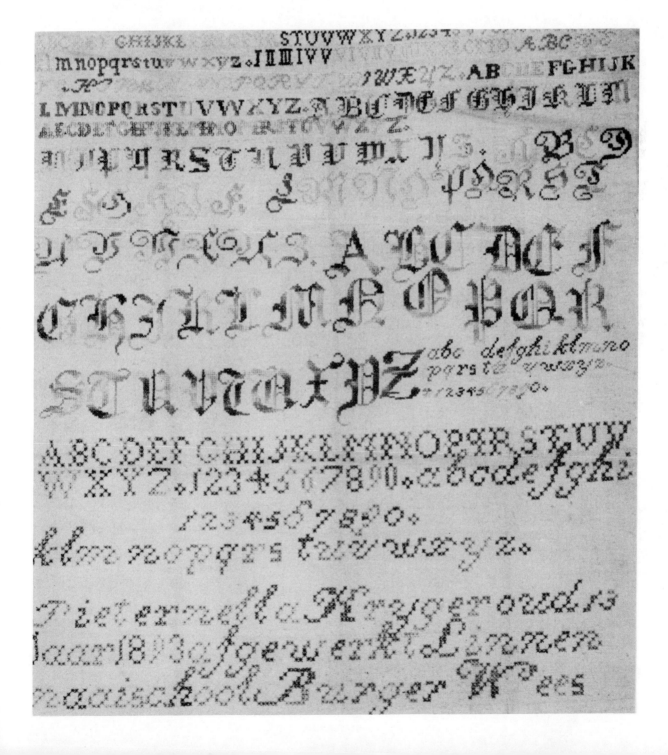

American sampler, dated 1764. (Courtesy of the Museum of Fine Arts, Boston, Massachusetts.)

Geographical Samplers

Embroidered geographical maps, which became the fashion in the eighteenth century (the English especially excelled in making these), might be called a borderline case of the sampler.

Initially, the maps were done by children, without a previous design of the country's outlines and specific areas on the material. This system, however, produced such curiously shaped maps that, soon, ready-made sampler patterns printed on linen or silk were customarily used.

There was an abundance of these maps in the latter half of the eighteenth century, frequently done in free embroidery, with the map at times surrounded by a wreath of flowers. With today's revival of almost all sampler forms, the geographical ones have followed the general trend, and among the countries where map samplers are produced (commercially, as well as individually) is Denmark. They are done mostly in the fine cross-stitch that is so typical for this country today, and space is left for the addition of names, dates, and other personal notes.

Map of Denmark measuring approximately 15 x 18 inches. (Courtesy of the Selskabet til Haandarbejdets Fremme, Copenhagen, Denmark.)

On the sampler above, Denmark is represented in delicate greens and blues on natural colored linen (not shown are Greenland and the Faeroe Islands).

Detail of a Denmark map as worked by the late Asta Hauch-Holm of Denmark and London, courtesy of Mr. and Mrs. Fleming Holm, London, England.

Danish Greenland is the subject of the sampler above, much more playful in character. The multicolored sampler includes a Greenland family, a variety of local flora and fauna, and an ever-shining sun that seems to be more wishful thinking than a representation of reality in that cold part of the world. The strictly geometrical border adds local atmosphere and forms a very unusual frame.

Danish artist Gerda Bengtsson designed a Thailand map with a delightful storytelling border: Bangkok's fabulous temples are represented, as are its famous local waterways (opposite page) that carry most merchandise to and from surrounding houses and farms. Traffic in some places there can be as dense as in midtown New York during the rush hours. The very simple wave pattern representing the various seas is particularly effective.

Map of Greenland. (Photo courtesy the Selskabet til Haandarbejdets Fremme, Copenhagen, Denmark.)

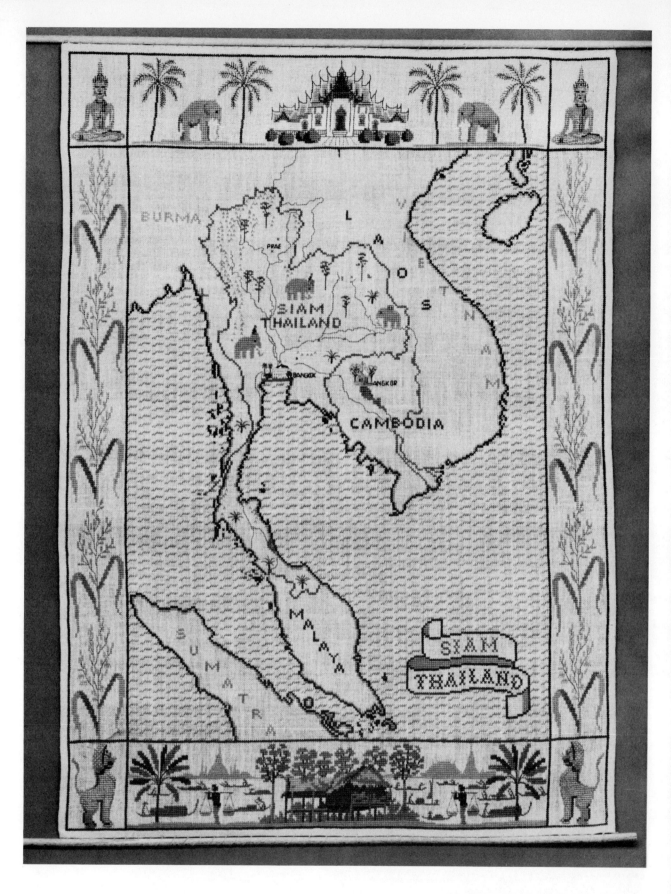

Map of Thailand and surrounding countries designed by Gerda Bengtsson. (Courtesy of the Selskabet til Haandarbejdets Fremme, Copenhagen, Denmark.)

An extraordinary, beautifully worked white-work sampler brings a map to mind in a very subtle, abstract manner. The technique is quite intricate: pieces of fine handkerchief lawn were inserted into a background of white linen. Various counted-thread stitches were combined with couched work, and details of closely worked French knots help give a three-dimensional aspect to this most unusual sampler.

The sampler is the work of a student at the Fine Art Department of London's Goldsmiths College, where — under Miss Constance Howard's guidance — many outstanding experiments in embroidery are being done.

Almost abstract, white-work map sampler, 1968, by Susan Kemp, student at Goldsmiths College, London, England; white on white linen, 13 x 10 inches.

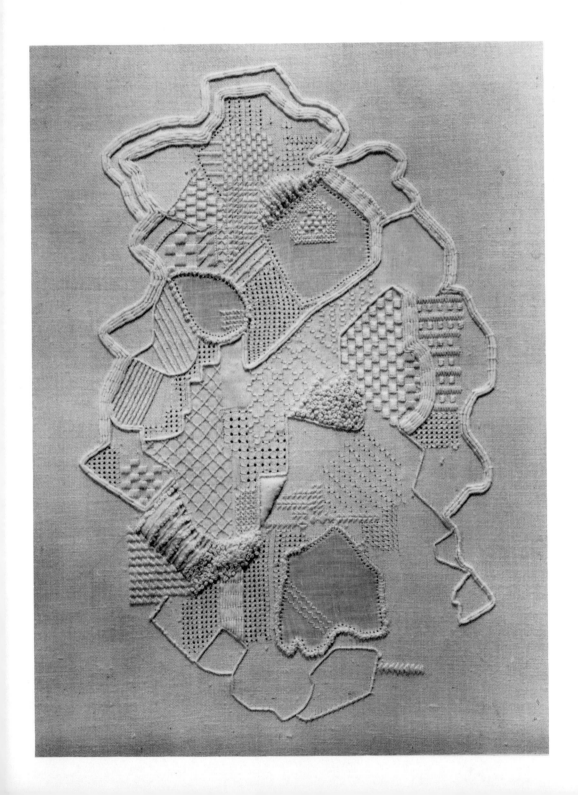

Blackwork is another technique that lends itself very well to the making of map samplers. The beautifully elaborate map of the United States not only has a different stitch for each of the states, but each state is named in the intricate border and identified by an accompanying repeat of its pattern. The map was worked with one strand of stranded cotton; border in matching pearl cotton with gold details.

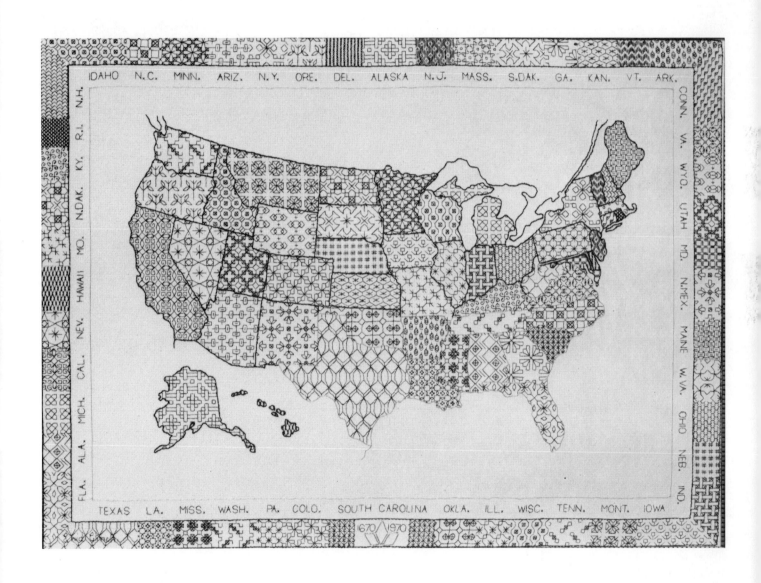

Sampler map of the United States in blackwork by Mrs. Harvey Clinch, an English lady who lives in South Carolina. First published in *Needle Arts,* the Embroiderers' Guild of America's publication. (Photo courtesy of Marion E. Scoular.)

Miss Nancy Maxwell embroidered the map of her native country, New Zealand, in a wide variety of blackwork stitches, combining this with very effectively placed "exercise" patterns. The work was done on an even-weave linen with black stranded and twisted silks and, except for a few darning and cross-stitch patterns, all stitches were worked in the backstitch — traditional for blackwork.

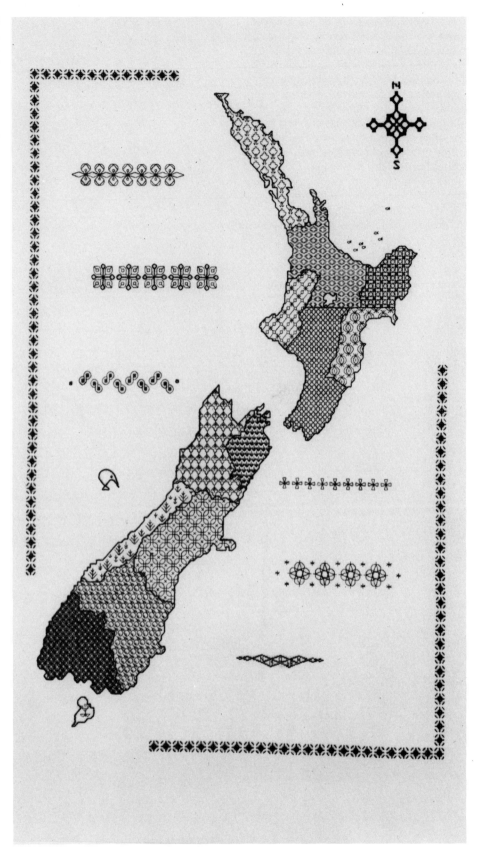

"The Dominion of Canada" is the work of Mrs. Kathleen Lymbery of the Crawford Bay's Women's Institute in Canada. (Crawford Bay is a small community in British Columbia, some 400 miles east of Vancouver.) The ten coats of arms of the different provinces are embroidered in vivid colors and surrounded by rows upon rows of stitch exercises in subdued background tones. The title at the top is in red; at the bottom, the Institute's motto, "For Home and Country," is in blue. A tiny segment of the Canada's Women's Institute, Crawford Bay (with ten members) is rightly proud of "their" sampler, which was a prize winner at a national exhibition.

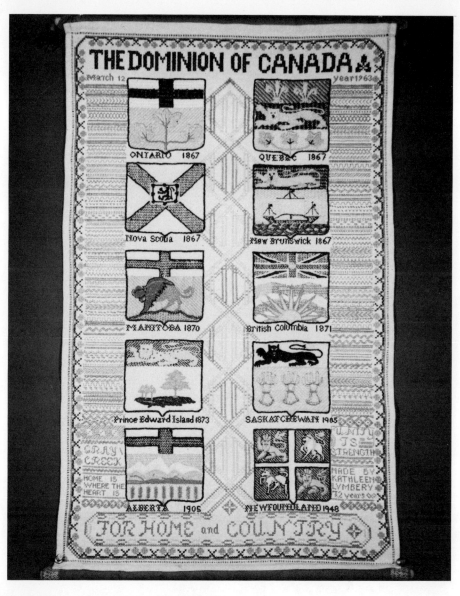

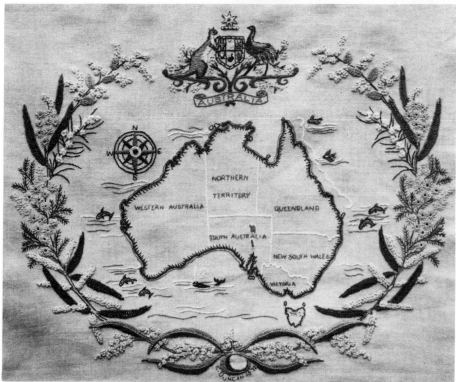

How many different ways there are of viewing one's country! Esme Duncan, a consummate embroideress, called her sampler "Australiana" and surrounded the map itself with a wreath of wattle, the Australian national flower.

A leading member and former president of Queensland's Embroiderers' Guild, Esme Duncan not only has won numerous prizes for her embroideries but has also taught music and art in various parts of her country. The size of her sampler is 21 x 17 inches; it was worked on pale blue linen with twisted and stranded cottons in many different colors and stitches. Although Mrs. Duncan had toyed for some time with the idea for this sampler, she completed it especially for inclusion in *Samplers for Today*.

3. Sources of Inspiration

Mrs. Patricia Cairns of Vancouver, B.C.,
Canada, took her inspiration from her
children's drawings.

Inspiration can come, literally, from anywhere, from anything, at any time. If you want to experiment in a special technique, such as crewel or couching, read a good book about it, study the history of it, and then decide whether you want to give your sampler a containing shape — such as a house, a country, an animal, or an abstract form — or whether you want it to be an exercise, pure and simple.

If you want to tell a story, there are endless sources to take your inspiration from; another embroidery or a painting, some historical document, or a pop-art drawing may be the thing that sets you on your way. This chapter is meant to emphasize the multitude of forms your sampler can take — forms that are different, unusual, in tune with our age or reminiscent of the past, big and bold or a minute masterpiece.

The main thing is to fix your choice and — please, please — select a technique that you enjoy working with, not only one that will look good when finished.

The shape your sampler is going to take is as important as your choice of technique. For instance, if you like to work in white on white, you might go in for an animal shape, such as this wonderfully cocky rooster.

White rooster worked on white tulle in different stitches with beads added, 1955. Designed by Elisabeth Geddes and worked by Mrs. G. Marriage, both of England. Size approximately 8½ x 8½ inches. (Collection Embroiderers' Guild, London, England.)

Design by Romualdo Scarpa and Serena Dal, executed at the Burano School, Burano, Italy. The piece won first prize at the Triennale IX in Milan. (Photograph by Mort Kaye.)

Or something like this modern, Italian lace panel might easily be translated into white embroidery and could prove to be your point of departure (opposite page).

A Danish sampler, showing a fascinating combination of counted-thread work (in this case mostly pulled work) and free embroidery patterns in white on white, might inspire you.

Danish sampler courtesy of the Arts and Crafts Museum, Copenhagen, Denmark; worked by Esther Faengel.

Extraordinary, multi-colored needle-lace borders from Greece provide delicate floral forms. The work is done without the aid of any lace pillow or other contraption, and it is used, among other things, to border scarves and belts with great effect.

Similarly, the needlework of other countries may stimulate ideas for sampler making. Here, a young Pakistani girl is learning her craft on a small embroidery hoop while, in Portugal, the women work together on a large frame to make a filet spread.

A Greek nun works on a flowered needle-lace border. (Photos by D.A. Harissiadis, Athens, Greece.)

Embroidery in Pakistan.

Filet work in Portugal.

You may want to follow a classical style, such as the one in this exercise sampler of satin stitch and eyelet embroidery, made in 1923 by a Norwegian girl (Signe Haugstoga). But, going further back in history, you may come across a more contemporary-looking inspiration, as this nineteenth-century Spanish sampler, with its Picasso-like moon that carelessly interrupts a serious sequence of stitch exercises.

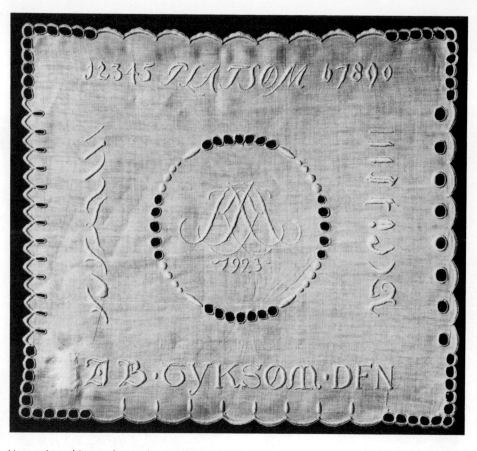

Norwegian white-work sampler, 1923. (Norsk Folkemuseum, Oslo, Norway).

Spanish nineteenth-century sampler on linen. (The Metropolitan Museum of Art, New York City, Rogers Fund, 1913.)

The array of fabulous mythological animals depicted on this extraordinary piece of textile, which is over 700 years old, could well inspire any present-day sampler enthusiast. Mythological subjects could be taken from books and other sources as well.

The Gösser Cope. Silk stitchery on white linen, Austria, circa 1230-1260. (Courtesy of the Osterreichisches Museum für Angewandte Kunst, Vienna, Austria. Photograph by Anton Fesl.)

Dr. Betty Grossman, program director of the St. Louis Art Museum and a highly knowledgeable woman with a seemingly insatiable thirst for further insight, at one time participated in excavations at Mycenae, and now owns a handbag depicting discoveries made there.

The handbag, designed by Susan Niekamp Hecker and made by Marian King Tichvinsky, represents ten objects and symbols that tell the Mycenae story. Shown on one side of the bag are: the Lion Gate that guards the citadel (which is where Dr. Grossman excavated), the Gold Diadem (one of Heinrich Schliemann's discoveries), a stirrup jug that was found in 1961 when Dr. Grossman worked there together with her husband, a plaster head that is considered the best existing representation of a Mycenaean face, and a terra cotta bull believed to be part of an ancient burial procedure.

On the other side of the handbag are: Gold Wheat (symbol of the goddess Demeter, whose artistic representations were the subject of Dr. Grossman's dissertation), the Octopus Vase (a famous local pottery find), the Goddess of Blessing as found represented on a Mycenaean gem, a Mother and Child terra cotta figurine (also locally excavated), and finally the famous Gold Mask that Schliemann believed to represent the face of Agamemnon.

The handbag, which measures approximately 9 x 12 inches, has a turquoise background and the various motifs are worked in colors as close as possible to those of the originals represented.

The scenes for an eighteenth-century Danish storytelling sampler were based on Biblical stories, which are also timeless in nature. Several segments depict Adam and Eve while additional sections give other Biblical details. The embroidery was done in red, yellow, brown, and green silks and spangles on a background of flax. (Museum Den Gamle By, Arhus, Denmark.)

"The Peaceable Kingdom," showing most stitches used in American crewel work. Designed by Doris Thacher; made by Kay Merill, both of New York State.

Sampler by Marian J. Metsopoulos of Lakewood, Colorado. Size 11½ x 18 inches, crewel wool and silk floss embroidery on linen. Named stitches illustrate the fillings used for the strawberries. (Pattern courtesy of Paragon Needlecraft, New York City.)

England's Pat Russell designed and made the children's alphabet panel. It measures 2 x 4 feet.

Rumāls, which roughly translated means "covering pieces," are East Indian storytelling samplers. On them, the East Indian woman depicts the story of her life or of a hunting party or of a mythological scene. As in the West, the work is sometimes signed by the maker. The two rumāls pictured here are from the valley of Chambā in the Western Himalayas. They are worked with silks in satin stitch (often double-sided) on fine hand-spun cotton.

The hunting scene shows the great variety of animals being chased and the many different weapons the hunters are using — a sword and shield, a spear, a bow and arrow, and a gun. (Size is approximately 32 inches square.) The marriage scene depicts an entire company of musicians, men with horses, an elephant, and a camel, as well as the nuptial bed, the presents received, and a host of traditional accessories for the ritual. The marriage pavilion occupies a center place and is surrounded by various deities. (Size is approximately 38 x 39 inches.)

East Indian storytelling samplers. (Both photographs courtesy of the Indian Museum, Calcutta, India.)

"Fishing Offshore" by Eufemia Espinosa.

Four examples of native embroidery from Black Island, Chile, on this page and top of opposite page. (Photographs courtesy of Mrs. Leonore Sobrino de Vera and the Sociedad de Arte Contemporaneo de Santiago, Chile.)

"Whale Catch" by Maria Luisa Alvarez.

"Grandmother Eating Maté" by Silvia Jofré.

"Wheat Threshing" by Transito Diaz.

Storytelling blanket with embroidered Hopi designs of three Kachinas, rain, and thunder symbols, from Pueblo, Arizona. (Kachinas are supernatural beings who visit Hopi villages during the first half of each year, bringing rain as well as gifts for the children.) Size: 58 x 72 inches. (Photograph courtesy of the Museum of the American Indian, Heye Foundation, New York City.)

In many countries, samplers (especially the storytelling ones) have taken different forms from those we are accustomed to in the Western world. Nevertheless, they serve exactly the same purpose, that of telling a story in small, unrelated figures.

The delightful pillow, or cushion, covering from the island of Skyros features a large ship manned by seamen. (This is a subject that is depicted on many samplers of my own native country, Holland, and recurs in many countries that are surrounded by water.) Here, the ship is accompanied by an incredible variety of fish, birds, men, flowers and sun-like motifs that, sampler-wise, fill up the entire background. The background is linen; the threads are of silk and cotton.

Detail of a modern Skyros embroidery, clearly showing the stitch that is so typical for the work of this island. (Author's collection.)

Cushion cover, Skyros, Greece. (Courtesy of the Benaki Museum, Athens, Greece.)

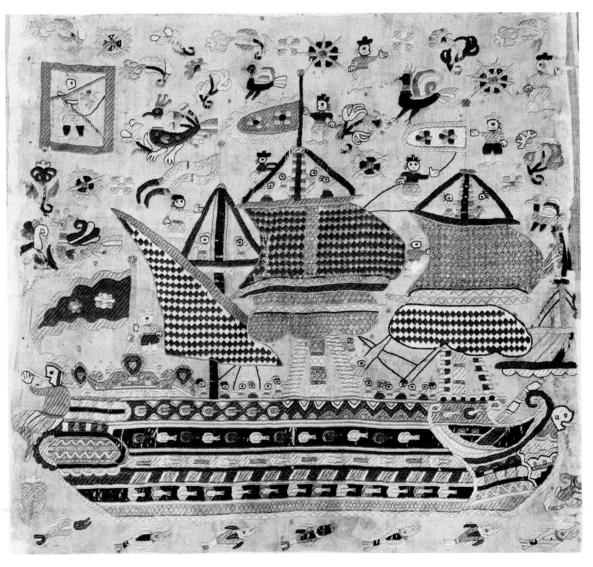

Cut and drawn-thread work. (Courtesy of the Victoria and Albert Museum, London, England.)

When looking at a design, it is not necessary to follow it precisely to execute it in embroidery; it is preferable to let one's imagination go to work and come to a personal solution.

Two examples, both done during the second half of the seventeenth century, illustrate how differently a similar motif can be handled. The example above is done in cutwork and drawn-thread work and shows two persons, presumably members of a royal family, under a canopy. The second example is an embroidered casket which, in the left-hand panel of the open view, shows an entirely different treatment of a like motif (below).

The closed view of the casket demonstrates how some of the motifs from the inner view have been transposed from flat embroidery into the typical stump work of seventeenth-century England. Sections of padded designs in high relief were combined with needle-lace detail added on top of the material to obtain a three-dimensional effect (opposite page).

English embroidered casket, circa 1670. (Both photographs courtesy of the Museum of Fine Arts, Boston, Massachusetts.)

Although appliqué work generally is not considered to be in the sampler's domain, there are often too many analogous elements to ignore its potential here. Appliqué work is one of the very oldest techniques known and therefore the fourteenth-century curtain detail shown here might be called a relative newcomer in the field. It is part of a patchwork appliqué work that, in some eighteen similar joint pieces, supposedly tells the story of a Sir Guy of Warwick. The exact origin of the work is not known but it is thought to be either French or English.

Detail of fourteenth-century appliqué curtain. (Courtesy of the Victoria and Albert Museum, London, England.)

How modern the appliqué quilt also shown here looks, and it is hard to imagine that it was made in Georgia in the U.S.A. around 1900. Only the costumes make it look different from the present-day appliqué hanging which comes from Dahomey, Africa. On second thought, in the latter, the animals do look slightly more ferocious.

Hanging from Dahomey, Africa. (Photo by Lee Brian, courtesy of the Hokin Gallery, Palm Beach, Florida.)

Appliqué quilt, circa 1900, from Georgia. (Museum of Fine Arts, Boston, Massachusetts.)

Much more sophisticated, a beautiful appliqué sampler-coverlet from England represents some twenty different species of birds, all nesting together in one single tree. The tree is surrounded by a sampler framework of different kinds of leaves.

This "nature lover's" piece is certainly not an ordinary, run-of-the-mill sampler; its size is 100 x 86 inches. It was done on unbleached calico in applied work, with the fine details such as beaks, legs and eyes added in embroidery. The design was made by England's Averil Colby and it was executed by Miss D.M. Crampton, in 1964.

The maker must have had a glorious time and a great love for the work at hand. She chose textures and colors of the applied patches to represent nature as closely as possible — and succeeded in this without overdoing her effects at any moment.

Appliqué coverlet from England. (Photograph courtesy of Miss Averil Colby and Miss D. M. Crampton.)

Another interesting technique, in which you may find you are particularly gifted, is needle painting — work done with irregular, straight stitches. The Chinese, amongst others, have specialized in a very delicate form of needle painting in silk.

Or your sampler might be inspired by this much bolder, Japanese work, done with appliqué and yielding an almost three-dimensional effect. (This detail, as well as the previous one, is from complete room furnishings presented to William V of the Netherlands in 1791.)

Detail from the Chinese Room in the Royal Palace "Huis ten Bosch," The Hague, the Netherlands. (By gracious permission of H.M. Queen Juliana of the Netherlands. Photograph by Frits Gerritsen.)

Detail from the Japanese Room in the Royal Palace "Huis ten Bosch," The Hague, the Netherlands (By gracious permission of H.M. Queen Juliana of the Netherlands. Photograph by Frits Gerritsen.)

135

A style of embroidery that seems to be catching on all over the world is one that is similar to the Grandma Moses-style in painting. Indeed, the use of this style would bring the design part of a picture-sampler within the reach of many an amateur. Shown on color page 126, the brightly colored wool embroideries worked by the women of Black Island, a Chilean fishing port, exemplify this style.

It was a Santiago pediatrician's wife, Mrs. Leonore Sobrino de Vera, who inspired the Black Island women to make more out of their traditional embroideries than just doilies. Slowly, at first, the women started depicting their daily life in small decorative embroideries: the baking day, the fishermen's adventures, and so forth. Their work pictures began to come alive, embroidered in brightly colored woolen yarn on cotton, until — not long ago — they were exhibited in Santiago's National Museum of Art. The technique is of very simple, straight stitches, which usually completely cover the cotton background. Very shortly we may see an international fame for these pictures, such as that achieved by the traditional "Molas" worked by the San Blas (Panama) embroideresses.

"Whale Catch" by Maria Luisa Alvarez. Embroidery from Black Island, Chile.

In Peru, a Peace Corps volunteer working in the village of Chijnaya hit on the idea of teaching the children there to embroider, using homespun wool from sheep and llamas. Soon, having learned only a few basic stitches, the children started to give their own, free and untaught vision of life at home.

Fishermen from the nearby lake, men at work in the fields, llamas and pigs, the sun, and their homes are the subjects that parade in vivid colors across their small, fascinating embroideries. Not only has the enterprise resulted in many hours of friendly competition and junior social gatherings amongst the children, but the sale of their products helps provide the village with books, shoes, building funds, etc.

Chijnaya child at work. (Photograph courtesy of the Andean Foundation, Washington, D.C.)

A storytelling sampler, size approximately 5 x 7 inches, from Chijnaya, Peru.

Boys as well as girls participate in their new-found sport. This one was made Eulojio M. (Photograph courtesy of the Smithsonian Institution, Washington, D.C., and the Andean Foundation.)

4. Stitches and Techniques

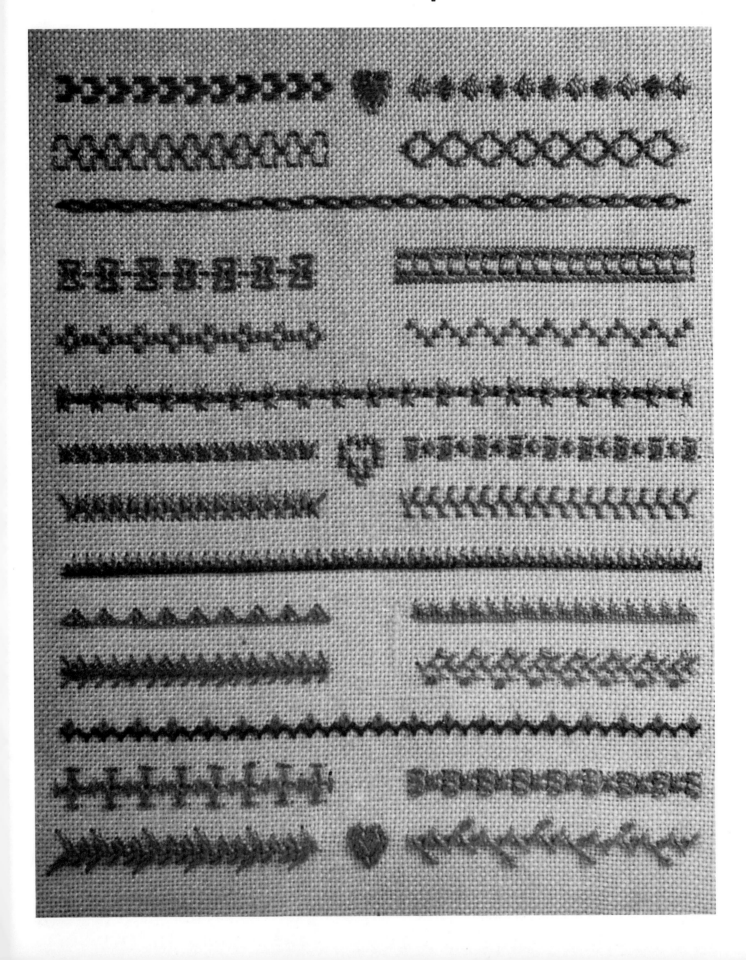

The Basics

All embroidery, and I really mean *all* embroidery, springs from a common source: the basic, utilitarian stitches that were invented when people started to wear clothes and this clothing needed fastening, finishing off, joining or repairing. Any sewing stitch done with the aim of decoration instead of pure utility becomes an embroidery stitch. Since all past and present-day embroidery stitches evolved from, or were in some way derived from, the same first attempts at stitched adornment, it seems only natural to go to these sources in order to find out how the incredible variety of embroidery stitches that we now possess came to grow and flourish.

On the following pages, groups of what I like to call "basic" stitches are given. The stitches and groups all relate to each other, grow out of each other, lead one to the other. In between and around the stitches I chose as examples, there are literally thousands of other varieties, adaptations, and combinations for anyone to freely experiment with in making a sampler of embroidery stitches.

I have avoided using any but the most basic name for each stitch, for this book is meant as an internationally orientated survey, and in many countries identical stitches are called by widely different, sometimes even contradicting, names.

The simplest of stitch samplers can have a definite visual appeal. Much depends on coloring, on grouping of stitches, on composition. This sampler was done in reds and greens (twisted cotton) on natural colored, fairly coarse, even-weave linen.

Straight stitches, worked simply from point A to point B, are the basis of roughly three-quarters of embroidery. The following techniques, to name but a few, rely on straight stitches: needle painting, blackwork, Holbein stitchery, pulled-fabric work, and drawn-thread work.

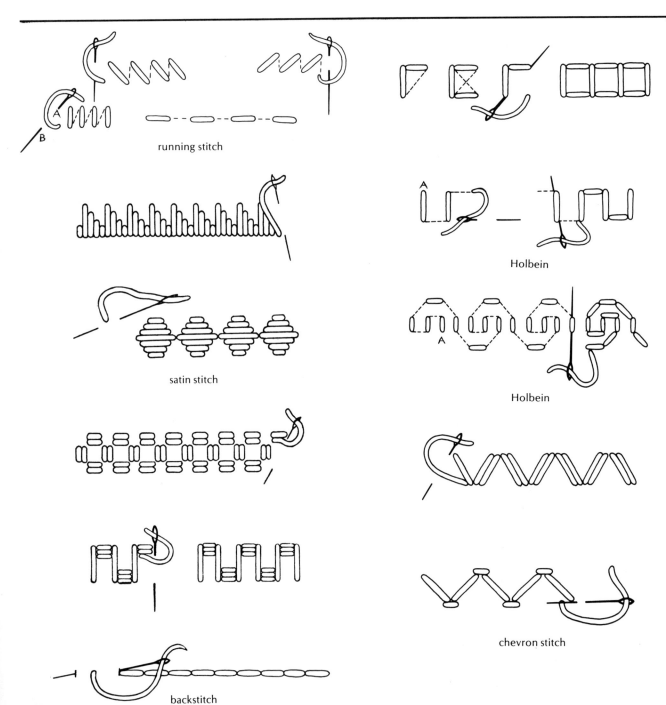

running stitch

Holbein

satin stitch

Holbein

chevron stitch

backstitch

Simple straight stitches may cross each other in a variety of ways, or they may have other straight stitches added to emphasize or enhance them. There is not just "the" cross-stitch, but a whole group of them. The use of one or the other depends on your personal choice of materials, stitch proportions, and combination of stitches appropriate for the design as well as on your free interpretation of each stitch idea.

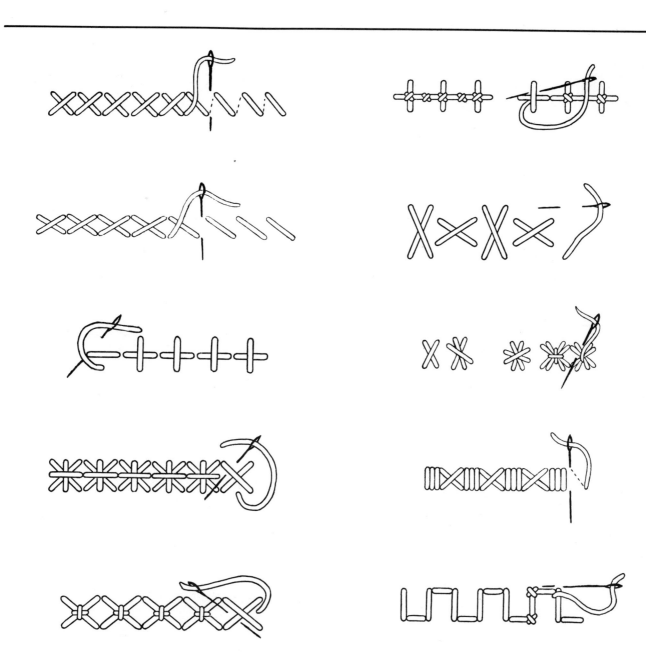

Instead of crossing each other completely, straight stitches may cross partially, as in herringbone stitches. Partially crossed stitches tend to form continuous rows rather than small, independent motifs (joined in some way or another) as is the case with completely crossed stitches.

Once again, there is an enormous variety of herringbone-type stitches, and these can also be combined with simple, straight stitches.

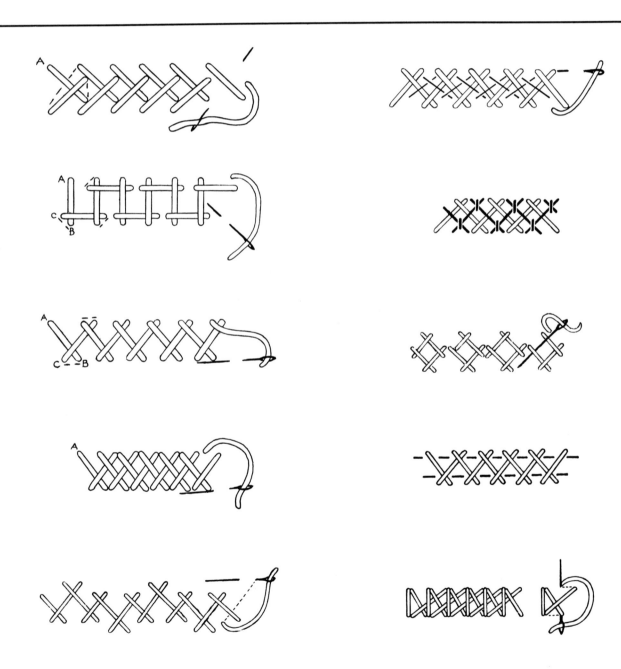

Stitchers found that by diverting the thread from a straight path a protective loop was formed which kept the material from getting frayed. That is how all buttonhole stitchery came into existence. The straight line between two points of the stitch was altered merely by pulling the thread under the needle point as it emerged from the third point of the stitch instead of leaving the thread above the needle point. To transform the herringbone stitch, the direction of the needle was changed from horizontal to vertical when going from the second point to the third point.

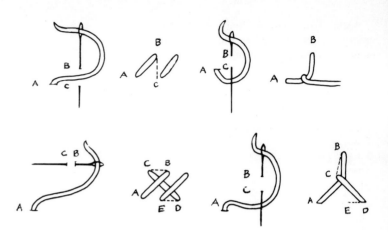

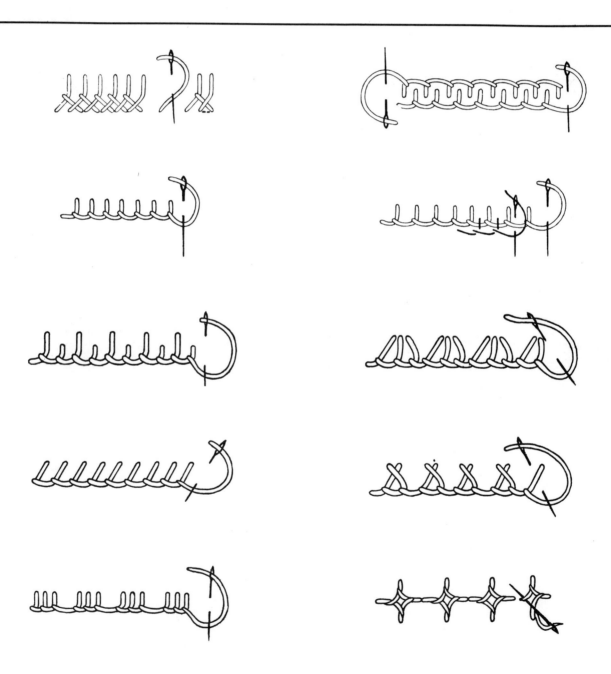

These buttonhole loops can be "closed down" to the left, until we arrive at the chain stitch, or opened up to the right until a stem stitch is the result.

All sorts of intermediate stitches (some called featherstitches, others open chain or fly stitches) lie within this realm and form part of the endless variations in embroidery.

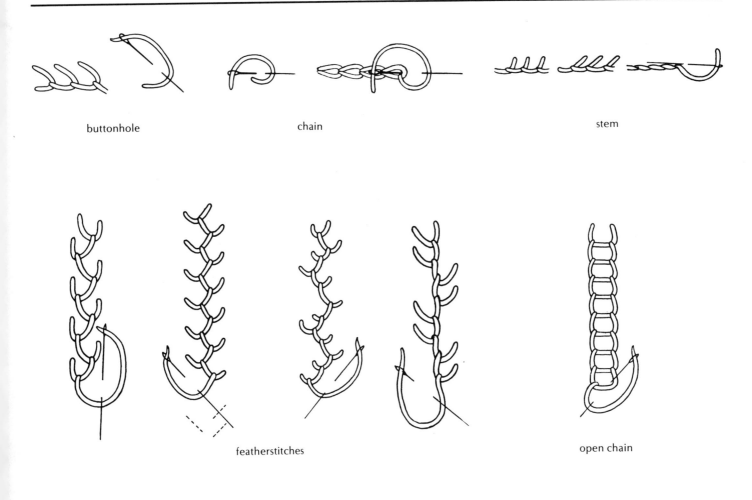

buttonhole   chain   stem

featherstitches   open chain

fly stitch   fly stitch

The chain-stitch possibilities, again, are infinite and lead us to more complicated twists with the needle, resulting in what — in my book — are called "magical stitches," for the results obtained are often totally unexpected and seem, but only seem, to have no relation with the stitch movements made.

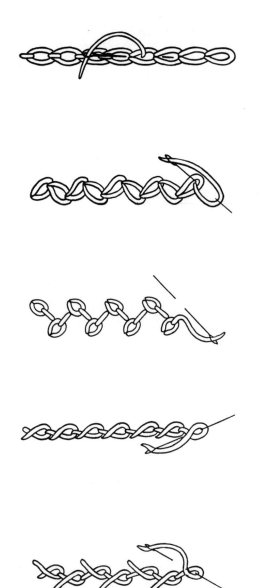

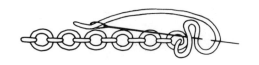

cable chain

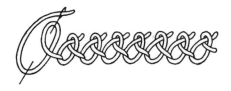

French knots

Many basic stitches can be given a complete face-lift, even a three-dimensional aspect in the following way. First, complete a row or pattern of the basic stitch. Then take a second thread (not necessarily the same color or thickness) and elaborate on the initial work, interlacing the new thread with the basic stitches. Do not pass the thread through the background material; use only the first stitches as a basis for further stitchery.

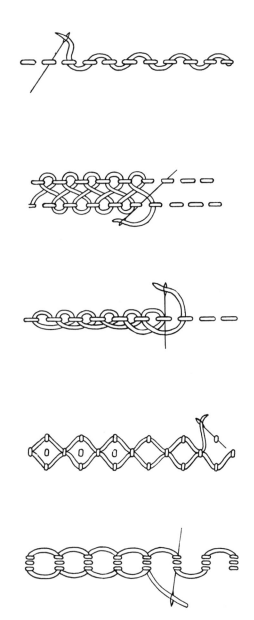

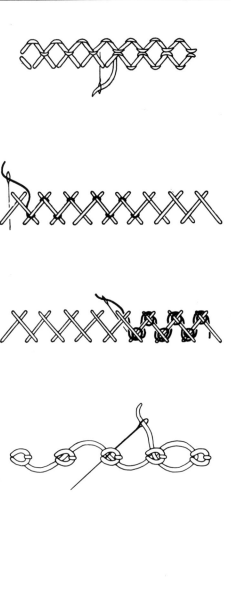

The Initial Choice

In what one might say is almost a reversal of the stitch technique just described, for couching, a thread, cord, or braid is laid on the material first and afterwards fixed onto the background by stitchery. There are many different kinds of couching — from the cord application of Eastern Europe and the Near East to the intricate silk work from Japan; from the stately, medieval gold and silk work of Western Europe to the simple sewing on of peasant braid. (See pages 58 to 61.)

Couching is very close to applied work. In the latter case, instead of applying a thread or cord, one applies a piece of material, which is sewn onto the background by various means of stitchery. (See pages 132 to 135.)

This leads, in turn, to applying non-textile objects to the background material, objects such as beads, precious stones, leather, shells, or feathers. What tremendous scope all this offers for experimenting. (See pages 98, 103, and 115.)

As mentioned previously, embroidery stitches can be worked onto a background in two different ways: the counted-thread method and the free embroidery method.

The first method relies on using the background material as a guideline and counting the threads of its weave so that embroidery and background are, to a certain extent, dependent on each other. Examples of techniques using the counted-thread method are: Holbein work, drawn- thread work, canvas work, and pulled-fabric work.

In the second method, the background material functions solely as a background for working the embroidery along predesigned or imaginary lines that are completely independent of the weave of the material. Examples of techniques using free embroidery are: needle painting, crewel work, satin stitch, modern Hedebø, and shadow work.

It is, of course, sometimes possible to combine both ways of working on one piece of material — at times following the weave, at other times ignoring it.

Some embroidery stitches (the cross-stitch, for example,) lend themselves more to counted-thread work. Others, such as the chain stitch, are easier to work along the lines of free embroidery. But most stitches are easily adaptable to both ways of working.

It is very important to find out which method of embroidery one is most gifted for, where one's best abilities lie. In my many years of teaching, I found people who are equally creative in both methods of work so rare as to be almost non-existent.

Some Identifiable Techniques

There is an incredible variety of ways in which people have — through many centuries and all over the world — adapted basic stitch possibilities to their climate, their available materials, and their tastes. Among the many techniques in existence, there are quite a few that have become universally recognizable and these are listed here alphabetically with a brief description of each one's characteristics. Pages on which examples of the technique appear are noted in parentheses.

Applied Work or Appliqué

Pieces of material cut to desired shapes are attached to a background and are sometimes outlined and further complemented by embroidery stitches. (See pages 132 to 135 and page 103.)

Blackwork

Mainly popular in England, where it already existed in the sixteenth century, blackwork is a counted-thread technique. It is traditionally worked in black on white, using mainly straight stitches such as Holbein and cross-stitches. (See pages 40, 41, 78, 111, and 112.)

Canvas Work

Worked on canvas mesh, there are a multitude of stitches, in addition to the traditional tent stitch and cross-stitch, which can be used. The stitches are worked so that the entire canvas is covered by yarn. (See pages 32 to 38.)

Couching

A cord or thread is laid on the material to follow a designed line, or to fill up parts of the background, and it is kept in place by stitches that fasten it to the material at intervals. These are mostly small, straight stitches (they often form a pattern in themselves), but sometimes chain stitches or cross-stitches are also used.

In a coarser form of couching, ribbons of material are laid on the background and fastened by decorative stitches, thus coming very near to the field of appliqué. Couching is often done in gold, in cord, and silk. (See pages 58 to 61, 98, 103, and 110.)

Crewel or Jacobean Work

This type of free embroidery is traditionally worked on linen or cotton "twill" with fine "crewel" wool and using "crewel" needles.

Crewel work originated in England in the seventeenth century, moved with the English settlers to North America, and has retained its popularity right up until today. That is no doubt due to the great variety of stitches used in it and the complete freedom of interpretation that it allows. Stitches include stem outline, long and short, chain, buttonhole, cross-stitch, French knot, herringbone, satin and seed. (See pages 93 and 123.)

Cutwork

Cutwork covers a multitude of possibilities. Open spaces are obtained by cutting away pieces of the material, or by piercing holes into it. The holes are carefully surrounded and protected by close buttonhole or overcast stitchery; the bigger spaces are filled in with needle-lace patterns. Often a combination of cutwork with free embroidery leads to spectacular results. Cutwork techniques include: *broderie anglaise*, Richelieu work, Venetian work, and modern Hedebø. (See pages 9, 10, and 129.)

Darning

Decorative darning is really darning the material without the necessity of doing so. Using parallel, sometimes interlacing rows of running stitches, beautiful geometric patterns can be achieved with entire patches of the new weave covering the material. Some embroidery materials (such as "huckaback") are made especially for decorative darning. (See page 39.)

Drawn-Thread Work

This technique consists of drawing some of the threads out of the background material, either in one or in both directions of the weave, and then grouping the remaining threads together in "bundles," by overcasting and needle weaving, to form a pattern. Filling stitches may be used in open spaces to obtain a lacelike effect. Hardanger work is one example of this. (See pages 10, 29, 30, 65, 78, 119, and 129.)

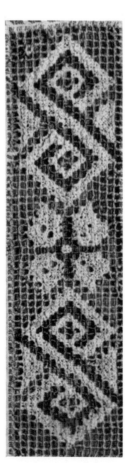

Filet Darning

As the name indicates, this is darning worked in running stitches on filet (a knotted, mesh fabric similar to but finer than fishermen's net). Although not very popular at present, there were times when this technique was every bit as much of a "rage" as canvas and crewel work are now. In the olden days, people even knotted their own filet fabric.

Holbein Work

Done traditionally in black on white, Holbein consists of small, straight running stitches worked across the material in one direction with the spaces between stitches filled in on the return journey, so that the end result is identical on the front and back of the material. (See page 8.)

Needle Painting

In this embroidery technique, work is done in straight stitches of uneven lengths and in irregular rows, shading the colors and directing the stitches to give an effect similar to that of a painter's brush. Their irregularity differentiates these stitches from the normal long and short stitches used in crewel work. (See pages 58 and 135.)

Net Embroidery

This is rather similar to filet darning except that it is worked on a background of much finer net, thus making more subtle effects possible.

Patchwork

Instead of being applied to an existing background, individual pieces of material are joined together to form a pattern. Many different kinds of material can be used, including printed ones. The plain sections of the material are often adorned with embroidery. (See page 79.)

Pulled-Fabric Work

This counted-thread technique is worked on a loosely woven, preferably even-weave material using tightly drawn stitches, mainly backstitches, to pull the material together at regular intervals and produce a pattern of tiny holes in it. The work is preferably done in thin threads of the same color of the material, since the aim is the lacelike transformation of the background. (See pages 78, 110, and 117.)

Quilting

In English quilting, two layers of material with a soft "padding" layer in between are joined by stitchery, either by hand or machine. In Italian quilting, the top and bottom layers are joined by stitches outlining the design, and the padding is then introduced between the outlines of that pattern. (See page 55.)

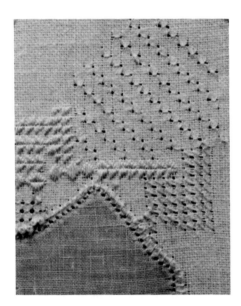

Shadow Work

One needs a transparent material to do this and the embroidery is worked from the back so that, apart from the stitches appearing on the front, the color of the embroidery thread behind highlights the material. When closed herringbone stitches are worked on the back, they appear as backstitches on the front.

Smocking

Because of its utilitarian aspects, smocking belongs more to the field of sewing than embroidery, although the two of them are frequently combined. It is a decorative method of gathering material into little tucks.

This short survey does not, by any means, imply that there are no other "identifiable" techniques. The Moroccan work shown in some detail on page 63 had its own characteristics; similarly there are also very typical embroideries from Rhodes, from Crete, from Hungary, and a hundred other places. Then there are historical techniques that are rarely, or never, used anymore: the famous stump work; the old, beautifully severe Hedebø style, Dresden work (a combination of pulled-fabric work within free embroidery shapes on very fine muslin) and many, many others.

Much of the joy of embroidery lies, it seems to me, in the endless possibilities it offers to the curious, the inventive, the adventurous mind. The particular joy of making a sampler lies in the fact that it can be built out of any one, or all, of these possibilities.

5. General Hints

This sampler has been framed behind glass, not to hang on the wall, but to serve as a table top. Design by Mazoltov was worked and added to by Mrs. Sibyl Golden of New York City.

The following are just a few points that are useful to bear in mind when making a sampler — or any embroidery for that matter:

1. Pointed needles, which are meant to pierce the threads of the woven background, are used when doing free embroidery; blunt needles are meant for passing the needle in between the threads of the woven background and are used for most counted-thread work.

2. If you are working a counted-thread embroidery and want to achieve a "square" look (with your horizontal stitches exactly the same size as the vertical ones) go for an "even-weave" material, which has identical threads for warp and woof.

3. If you are making your sampler not as a sample for future work but for its own decorative value, be sure to organize it beforehand, so that there is enough material left on all sides for whatever seam or mounting that has to be done upon completion.

4. If the sampler is meant for one particular place in the home, try and work the colors so that they either recall or offset the room's general color scheme.

5. Don't do as the Moroccans tend to do, but choose a background material worthy of all the leisure time to be put into your sampler.

6. If you are going to work a canvas sampler in tent stitches, remember that the European way of working it in horizontal rows (Continental stitch) has a tendency to deform the canvas more than the American way, which is generally based on diagonal rows of the tent stitch (basket weave stitch). On the other hand, many people find the working of the Continental stitch easier on the eye. In any case, consult a good, basic book on needlepoint or canvas work for explanations regarding blocking (bringing the finished work back to its intended shape).

7. The use of some kind of embroidery frame is indispensable for several techniques such as cutwork, drawn-thread work and needle painting; however, do not use one indiscriminately, for you may find that your particular eyes and hands work better without a frame.

8. When you sit down to work, try and relax. Seat yourself in a position that gives you full and efficient use of your hands and eyes but leaves all unneeded muscles at rest. Make sure that the light you use does not cast shadows between you and your work.

9. Good embroidery scissors should have sharp, preferably long, points; do not economize when buying them.

10. All needles have a tendency to rust under certain climatic conditions. *Never* leave one in a visible spot on your work but take it out, or pass it through the reverse side of your stitches, when you stop work.

11. I am a convinced believer in the use of a thimble; it is an absolutely necessary protective device and you should start using one right this minute, even though it may take a little time to accustom yourself to it.

12. Remember, please, that embroidery in general, and sampler making in particular, is supposed to be a joy, not an aggravating task that you set yourself to accomplish. The hours spent in making a sampler should be enjoyed every bit as much as the time spent looking at the finished product.

13. Once the sampler is finished, it can either be mounted as a wall panel or fashioned into a functional object. Work towards the end result from the beginning. The following are some suggestions of objects for which samplers are suitable:
a belt
a scroll
a box
a footstool
a handbag
a pincushion
a book cover
a bed cover
a chair cushion or cover
a frame
a screen or divider
a paperweight
a desk set
a tabletop
a pillow
a rug
Or maybe you would like to invent another "thingy," in the style of the turtle on page 42, like a giraffe, or, perhaps, a mock bottle to stand somewhere, or a puppet on a string.

6. Mounting a Sampler

When all is said and done, one of the most effective uses of a sampler is as a wall panel. If you want yours to be truly effective, and to keep its shape forever, this is what you do:

Have a piece of Masonite cut to size according to the sampler's dimensions, allowing a margin of material all around the sampler to overlap the panel. A 1/8-inch thick board is sufficient unless the sampler is unusually large, in which case take the next thickness of Masonite. Cut a piece of thin "art foam" approximately 1-inch wider on all sides than the Masonite panel is. Place the panel on top of the foam and cover the outside borders on the rear of the panel with a thinnish layer of textile glue.

When the glue begins to set, fold the protruding edges of the foam over, carefully stretching the foam a little so that there are no wrinkles or other uneven spots in the foam covering the front of the panel. Cut away surplus materials at the corners. Allow the panel to dry, first turning it over so the foam-covered side is face up and weighting it with some heavy books.

Then put the sampler in place on the front of the panel. Turn the panel rear side up again, fold the margins of fabric over and pin them to the panel along the edges. Thread a needle with strong embroidery thread and stitch from margin to margin, stretching the thread across the back of the panel in two directions, as shown. The stitches should be no more than 1/8 of an inch apart, and the thread (nr. 12 is good) should be pulled taut with each stitch. Take special care to make the corners look neat. After this, the panel can be hung as it is, or it can be finished with cord or braid at the edges, or it can be framed.

If your sampler is of a fragile nature (with a thin background material, for instance, or containing a lot of openwork), just sew the finished and hemmed sampler onto a stronger background; then, leaving none, or as much of this new background as desired showing, proceed as outlined above.

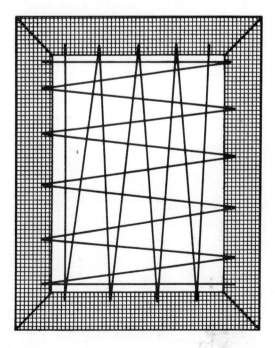

Mrs. Daryl Parshall of Millbrook, New York, embroidered the silk bird-study panel (designed by Erica Wilson) and mounted it in a unique way (size is 20 x 40 inches).

Books to Read and Keep

This is by no means a complete survey but rather a small and personal choice of books to help you on your way. The books marked with an asterisk (*) are somewhat older and may or may not be readily available.

General Knowledge

Bargello. Elsa Williams. Van Nostrand Reinhold Company, New York, 1967.

Embroidery. Cécile Dreesmann. MacMillan, New York, 1970.

Embroidery Book. Mary Thomas. Hodder & Stoughton, Ltd., London, 1936.

Encyclopedia of Needlework. Thérèse de Dillmont. Librairie Ch. Delagrave, Paris.

Inspiration for Embroidery. Constance Howard. B.T. Batsford, Ltd., London, 1966.

The Stitches of Creative Embroidery. Jacqueline Enthoven. Van Nostrand Reinhold Company, New York, 1964.

Specific Subjects

American Crewel Embroidery. Muriel Baker. Charles E. Tuttle Co., Rutland, and Tokyo, 1966.

Bead Embroidery. Joan Edwards. B.T. Batsford Ltd., London, 1966.

Blackwork Embroidery. Geddes & McNeill. Mills & Boon, Ltd., London, 1965.

Drawn Fabric Embroidery. Agnes M. Leach. Edward Hulton, London, 1959.

Ecclesiastical Embroidery. Meryl Dean. B.T. Batsford Ltd., London, 1958.

Lettering for Embroidery. Pat Russell. B.T. Batsford Ltd., London, and Van Nostrand Reinhold Company, New York, 1971.

Machine Embroidery. Jennifer Gray. B.T. Batsford Ltd., London, 1963.

Metal Thread Embroidery. Barbara Dawson. B.T. Batsford Ltd., London, 1968.

Needlepoint. Hope Hanley. Faber and Faber Ltd., London, 1964.

Needlepoint Design. Louis J. Gartner Jr. William Morrow & Company, New York, 1970.

Patchwork. Averil Colby. B.T. Batsford Ltd., London, 1958.

Stitchery for Children. Jacqueline Enthoven. Van Nostrand Reinhold Company, New York, 1968.

The Art of Crewel Embroidery. Mildred J. Davis. Vista Books, London, 1962.

The Romance of the Patchwork Quilt in America. Carrie Hall and Rose G. Kretsinger. The Caxton Printers, Ltd., Caldwell, 1947.

Traditional Quilting. Mavis Fitzrandolph. B.T. Batsford Ltd., London, 1954.

Bibliography

Alford, Lady M. *Needlework as Art*. London: Sampson Low, Marston, Searle and Rivington, 1886.

Ashton, Leigh. *Samplers*. London; Boston: The Medici Society, 1926.

Bhattacharyya, A.K. *Chambā Rumāl*. Calcutta: Indian Museum, 1968.

Bolton; Coe. *American Samplers*. Massachusetts Society of Colonial Dames, 1921.

Bottema, Hil. *Merklappen, Oud en Nieuw*. Kampen: J.H. Kok, 1942.

Butler, Jacqueline. *Yao Design*. Bangkok: The Siam Society, 1970.

Colby, Averil. *Samplers*. London: B.T. Batsford, Ltd., 1964.

Cordry, Donald and Dorothy. *Mexican Indian Costumes*. Austin; London: University of Texas Press, 1968.

Elyin, M. *Russian Decorative Folk Art*. Moscow: Foreign Languages Publishing House, 1959.

Fél, Edit; Hofer, Tamás; Csilléry, Klára K. *Hungarian Peasant Art*. Budapest: Corvina, 1958.

Gayot, H., and Mme. Minault. *La Broderie de Fès*. Rabat: Ecole du Livre, 1959.

-------. *La Broderie de Meknès*. Rabat: Ecole du Livre, 1959.

Harbeson, Georgiana Brown. *American Needlework*. New York: Coward-McCann, Inc., 1938.

Hughes, Therle. *English Domestic Needlework*. London: Lutterworth Press, 1961.

Huish, Marcus B. *Samplers and Tapestry Embroideries*. London: The Fine Art Society; New York and Bombay: Longmans, Green and Co., 1900; New York: Dover, 1970.

Jones, Mary Eirwen. *British Samplers*. Oxford: Pen in Hand Publishing Co., 1948.

King, Donald. *Samplers*. London: Victoria and Albert Museum, 1960.

Mehta, Rustam J. *Masterpieces of Indian Textiles*. Bombay: D.B. Taraporevala Sons & Co., Private Ltd., 1970.

Minnich, Helen Benton. *Japanese Costume and the Makers of Its Elegant Tradition*. Rutland; Tokyo: Charles E. Tuttle Co., 1963.

National Museum of Wales; Press Board of the University of Wales. *Guide to the Collection of Samplers and Embroideries*. Cardiff: 1939.

Philadelphia Museum of Art. *The Story of Samplers*. Philadelphia: 1971.

Ricci, Elsa. *Ricami Italiani Antichi e Moderni*. Firenze: Felice le Monnier, 1925.

Schiffer, Margaret B. *Historical Needlework of Pennsylvania*. New York: Charles Scribner's Sons, 1968.

Schuette, Marie, and Muller-Christensen, Sigrid. *Das Stickereiwerk*. Tubingen: Verlag Ernst Wasmuth, 1965.

Segura Lacomba, Maravillas. *Bordados Populares Españoles*. Madrid: Instituto San José de Calasanz de Pedogogía, 1949.

Symonds, Mary, and Preece, Louisa. *Needlework Through the Ages*. London: Hodder & Stoughton, Ltd., 1928.

Tyrrell, Barbara. *Tribal Peoples of Southern Africa*. Capetown: Books of Africa (Pty.) Ltd., 1968.

Voorbergh, Cruys. *Erfenis van Eeuwen*. Amsterdam: N.V. De Arbeiderspers, 1941.

Wace, A.J.B. *Mediterranean and Near Eastern Embroideries*. London: Halton & Company, Ltd., 1935.

Photography Credits

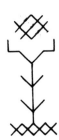

I asked the embroideress:
"Why is the last little animal not worked
as beautifully as the others?"

And she answered:
"One of them must always be left like that
so as not to irritate the Gods, for perfection
is Theirs alone."

from André Malraux: *Anti-Memoires*